BOOK OF
RHYMES

BOOK OF RHYMES

The Poetics of Hip Hop

Adam Bradley

BASIC
CIVITAS
BOOKS

A Member of the Perseus Books Group
New York

Books published by BasicCivitas are available at special discounts for bulk purchases
in the United States by corporations, institutions, and other organizations. For
more information, please contact the Special Markets Department at the
Perseus Books Group, 2300 Chestnut Street, Suite 200, Philadelphia, PA 19103,
or call (800) 810-4145, ext. 5000, or e-mail special.markets@perseusbooks.com.

Designed by Pauline Brown

Library of Congress Cataloging-in-Publication Data
Bradley, Adam.
Book of rhymes : the poetics of hip hop / by Adam Bradley.
p. cm.
Includes bibliographical references and index.
ISBN 978-0-465-00347-1 (alk. paper)
1. Rap (Music)—History and criticism. I. Title.
ML3531.B73 2009
782.421649—dc22
2008040250

10 9 8 7 6 5 4 3 2 1

To my mother,
Jane Louise Bradley,
who introduced me
to the poetry of music.

Contents

Prologue

This is hip hop. You are in a small club, standing room only. Maybe it's the Roots or Common or some underground group about to perform. Bodies press tightly against you. Blue wreaths of smoke hang just above your head. From the four-foot speakers at the front of the stage, you hear the DJ spinning hip-hop classics— A Tribe Called Quest, De La Soul, Rakim—charging the crowd as it waits, five minutes, ten minutes, longer, for the show to begin.

As the music fades to silence, a disembodied voice over the PA system announces the headliner. Lights grow warm, blue turns to yellow, then to red. The first beat hits hard, and the crowd roars as the MC—the rapper, hip hop's lyrical master of ceremonies—glides to the front of the stage. Hands reach for the sky. Heads bob to the beat. The crowd is a living thing, animated by the rhythm. It can go on like this for hours.

Now imagine this. It happens just as the performance reaches its peak. First the melody drops out, then the bass, and finally the drums. The stage is now silent and empty save for a lone MC, kicking rhymes a cappella. His voice fades from a shout to a whisper, then finally to nothing at all. As he turns to leave, you notice something stranger still: lyrics projected in bold print against the back of the stage. It's like you're looking directly into an MC's book of rhymes. The words scroll along in clear, neat lines against the wall. People stand amazed. Some begin to boo. Some start to leave.

But you remain, transfixed by the words. You notice new things in the familiar lyrics: wordplay, metaphors and similes, rhymes upon rhymes, even within the lines. You notice structures and forms, sound and silence. You even start to hear a beat; it comes from the language itself, a rhythm the words produce in your mind. You're bobbing your head again. People around you, those who remain, are doing it too. There's a group of you, smaller than before but strong, rocking to an inaudible beat.

The change is subtle at first. Maybe it's a stage light flickering back to life. Maybe it's a snare hit punctuating that inaudible rhythm. But now the lights burn brighter, the beat hits harder than ever, the MC bounds back on stage, the crowd reaches a frenzy. It's the same song, just remixed.

Through the boom of the bass you can still somehow hear the low rhythm the words make. Lines of lyrics pass across your mind's eye while the sound from the speakers vibrates your eardrums. For the first time you see how the two fit together—the sight and the sound. Rap hasn't changed, but you have. This is the poetry of hip hop.

Rap Poetry 101

I start to think and then I sink
into the paper like I was ink.
When I'm writing I'm trapped in between the lines,
I escape when I finish the rhyme . . .
—Eric B. & Rakim, "I Know You Got Soul"

A BOOK OF rhymes is where MCs write lyrics. It is the basic tool of the rapper's craft. Nas raps about "writin' in my book of rhymes, all the words pass the margin." Mos Def boasts about sketching "lyrics so visual / they rent my rhyme books at your nearest home video." They both know what Rakim knew before them, that the book of rhymes is where rap becomes poetry.

Every rap song is a poem waiting to be performed. Written or freestyled, rap has a poetic structure that can be reproduced, a deliberate form an MC creates for each rhyme that differentiates it, if only in small ways, from every other rhyme ever conceived. Like all poetry, rap is defined by the art of the line. Metrical poets choose the length of their lines to correspond to particular rhythms—they write in iambic pentameter or whatever other meter suits their desires. Free verse poets employ conscious line breaks to govern the reader's pace, to emphasize particular words, or to accomplish any one of a host of other poetic objectives. In a successful poem, line breaks are never casual or accidental. Rewrite a poem in prose and you'll see it deflate like a punctured lung, expelling life like so much air.

Line breaks are the skeletal system of lyric poetry. They give poems their shape and distinguish them from all other forms of literature. While prose writers usually break their lines wherever the page demands—when they reach the margin, when the computer drops their word to the next line—poets claim that power for themselves, ending lines in ways that underscore the specific design of their verse. Rap poets are no different.

Rap is poetry, but its popularity relies in part on people not recognizing it as such. After all, rap is for good times; we play it in our cars, hear it at parties and at clubs. By contrast, most people associate poetry with hard work; it is something to be studied in school or puzzled over for hidden insights. Poetry stands at an almost unfathomable distance from our daily lives, or at least so it seems given how infrequently we seek it out.

This hasn't always been the case; poetry once had a prized place in both public and private affairs. At births and deaths, weddings and funerals, festivals and family gatherings, people would recite poetry to give shape to their feelings. Its relative absence today says something about us—our culture's short attention span, perhaps, or the dominance of other forms of entertainment—but also about poetry itself. While the last century saw an explosion of poetic productivity, it also marked a decided shift toward abstraction. As the poet Adrian Mitchell observed, "Most people ignore poetry because most poetry ignores most people."

Rap never ignores its listeners. Quite the contrary, it aggressively asserts itself, often without invitation, upon our consciousness. Whether boomed out of a passing car, played at a sports stadium, or piped into a mall while we shop, rap is all around us. Most often, it expresses its meaning quite plainly. No expertise is required to listen. You don't need to take an introductory course or read a handbook; you don't need to watch an instructional video or follow an online tutorial. But, as with most things in life, the pleasure to be gained from rap increases exponentially with just a little studied attention.

Rap is public art, and rappers are perhaps our greatest public poets, extending a tradition of lyricism that spans continents and stretches back thousands of years. Thanks to the engines of global commerce, rap is now the most widely disseminated poetry in the history of the world. Of course, not all rap is great poetry, but collectively it has revolutionized the way our culture relates to the spoken word. Rappers at their best make the familiar unfamiliar through rhythm, rhyme, and wordplay. They refresh the language by fashioning patterned and heightened variations of everyday speech. They expand our understanding of human experience by telling stories we might not otherwise hear. The best MCs— like Rakim, Jay-Z, Tupac, and many others—deserve consideration alongside the giants of American poetry. We ignore them at our own expense.

Hip hop emerged out of urban poverty to become one of the most vital cultural forces of the past century. The South

Bronx may seem an unlikely place to have birthed a new movement in poetry. But in defiance of inferior educational opportunities and poor housing standards, a generation of young people—mostly black and brown—conceived innovations in rhythm, rhyme, and wordplay that would change the English language itself. In *Can't Stop, Won't Stop: A History of the Hip-Hop Generation*, Jeff Chang vividly describes how rap's rise from the 1970s through the early 1980s was accompanied by a host of social and economic forces that would seem to stifle creative expression under the weight of despair. "An enormous amount of creative energy was now ready to be released from the bottom of American society," he writes, "and the staggering implications of this moment eventually would echo around the world." As one of the South Bronx's own, rap legend KRS-One, explains, "Rap was the final conclusion of a generation of creative people oppressed with the reality of lack."

Hip hop's first generation fashioned an art form that draws not only from the legacy of Western verse, but from the folk idioms of the African diaspora; the musical legacy of jazz, blues, and funk; and the creative capacities conditioned by the often harsh realities of people's everyday surroundings. These artists commandeered the English language, the forms of William Shakespeare and Emily Dickinson, as well as those of Sonia Sanchez and Amiri Baraka, to serve their own expressive and imaginative purposes. Rap gave voice to a group hardly heard before by America at large, certainly never heard in their own often profane, always assertive words. Over time, the poetry and music they made would command the ears of their block, their borough, the nation, and eventually the world.

While rap may be new-school music, it is old-school poetry. Rather than resembling the dominant contemporary form of free verse—or even the freeform structure of its hiphop cousin, spoken word, or slam poetry, rap bears a stronger affinity to some of poetry's oldest forms, such as the strong-stress meter of *Beowulf* and the ballad stanzas of the bardic past. As in metrical verse, the lengths of rap's lines are governed by established rhythms—in rap's case, the rhythm of the beat itself.

The beat in rap is poetic meter rendered audible. Rap follows a dual rhythmic relationship whereby the MC is liberated to pursue innovations of syncopation and stress that would sound chaotic without the regularity of the musical rhythm. The beat and the MC's flow, or cadence, work together to satisfy the audience's musical and poetic expectations: most notably, that rap establish and maintain rhythmic patterns while creatively disrupting those patterns, through syncopation and other pleasing forms of rhythmic surprise.

Simply put, a rap verse is the product of one type of rhythm (that of language) being fitted to another (that of music). Great pop lyricists, Irving Berlin or John Lennon or Stevie Wonder, match their words not only to the rhythm of the music, but to melodies and harmonies as well. For the most part, MCs need concern themselves only with the beat. This fundamental difference means that MCs resemble literary poets in ways that most other songwriters do not. Like all poets, rappers write primarily with a beat in mind. Rap's reliance on spare, beat-driven accompaniment foregrounds the poetic identity of the language.

Divorced from most considerations of melody and harmony, rap lyrics are liberated to live their lives as pure expressions of poetic and musical rhythm. Even when rap employs rich melodies and harmonies—as is often the case, for instance, in the music of Kanye West—rhythm remains the central element of sound. This puts rap's dual rhythms in even closer proximity to one another than they might usually be in other musical genres. Skilled MCs underscore the rhythm of the track in the rhythm of their flows and the patterns of their rhymes. As a consequence, the lyrics rappers write are more readily separated from their specific musical contexts and presented in written form as poetry. The rhythm comes alive on the page because so much of it is embedded in the language itself.

Many of the reasonable arguments critics offer to distinguish musical lyrics from literary poetry do not apply to rap. One of the most common objections, voiced best by the critic Simon Frith, is that musical lyrics do not need to generate the highly sophisticated poetic effects that create the "music" of verse written for the page. Indeed, the argument goes, if a lyric is too poetically developed it will likely distract from the music itself. A good poem makes for a lousy lyric, and a great lyric for a second-rate poem. Rap defies such conventional wisdom. By unburdening itself from the requirements of musical form, rap is free to generate its own poetic textures independent of the music. Another objection is that popular lyric lacks much of the formal structure of literary verse. Rap challenges this objection as well by crafting intricate structures of sound and rhyme, creating some of the most scrupulously formal poetry composed today.

Rap's poetry can usefully be approached as literary verse while still recognizing its essential identity as music. There's no need to disparage one to respect the other. In fact, perhaps more than any other lyrical form, rap demands that we acknowledge its dual identity as word and song.

The fact that rap is music does not disqualify it as poetry; quite the contrary, it asserts rap's poetic identity all the more. The ancient Greeks called their lyrical poetry *ta mele*, which means "poems to be sung." For them and for later generations, poetry, in the words of Walter Pater, "aspires towards the condition of music." It has only been since the early twentieth century that music has taken a backseat to meaning in poetry. As the poet Edward Hirsch writes, "The lyric poem always walks the line between speaking and singing. . . . Poetry is not speech exactly—verbal art is deliberately different than the way that people actually talk—and yet it is always in relationship to speech, to the spoken word."

Like all poetry, rap is not speech exactly, nor is it precisely song, and yet it employs elements of both. Rap's earliest performers understood this. On "Adventures of Super Rhymes (Rap)" from 1980, just months after rap's emergence on mainstream radio, Jimmy Spicer attempted to define this new form:

It's the new thing, makes you wanna swing
While us MCs rap, doin' our thing
It's not singin' like it used to be
No, it's rappin' to the rhythm of the sure-shot beat
It goes one for the money, two for the show
You got my beat, now here I go

Rap is an oral poetry, so it naturally relies more heavily than literary poetry on devices of sound. The MC's poetic toolbox shares many of the same basic instruments as the literary poet's, but it also includes others specifically suited to the demands of oral expression. These include copious use of rhyme, both as a mnemonic device and as a form of rhythmic pleasure; as well as poetic tropes that rely upon sonic identity, like homonyms and puns. Add to this those elements the MC draws from music—tonal quality, vocal inflection, and so forth—and rap reveals itself as a poetry uniquely fitted to oral performance.

Earlier pop lyricists like Cole Porter or Lorenz Hart labored over their lyrics; they were not simply popular entertainers, they were poets. Great MCs represent a continuation and an amplification of this vital tradition of lyrical craft. The lyrics to Porter's "I Got You Under My Skin" are engaging when read on the page without their melodic accompaniment; the best rap lyrics are equally engrossing, even without the specific context of their performances. Rap has no sheet music because it doesn't need it—rapping itself rarely has harmonies and melodies to transcribe—but it *does* have a written form worth reconstructing, one that testifies to its value, both as music and as poetry. That form begins with a faithful transcription of lyrics.

Rap lyrics are routinely mistranscribed, not simply on the numerous websites offering lyrics to go, but even on an artist's own liner notes and in hip-hop books and periodicals. The same rhyme might be written dozens of different ways— different line breaks, different punctuation, even different words. The goal should be to transcribe rap verses in such a way that they represent on the page as closely as possible what we hear with our ears.

The standardized transcription method proposed here may differ from those used by MCs in their own rhyme books. Tupac, for instance, counted his bars by couplets. Rappers compose their verses in any number of ways; what they write need only make sense to them. But an audience requires a standardized form organized around objective principles rather than subjective habits. Serious readers need a common way of transcribing rap lyrics so that they can discuss rap's formal attributes with one another without confusion.

Transcribing rap lyrics is a small but essential skill, easily acquired. The only prerequisite is being able to count to four in time to the beat. Transcribing lyrics to the beat is an intuitive way of translating the lyricism that we hear into poetry that we can read, without sacrificing the specific relationship of words to music laid down by the MC's performance. By preserving the integrity of each line in relation to the beat, we give rap the respect it deserves as poetry. Sloppy transcriptions make it all but impossible to glean anything but the most basic insights into the verse. Careful ones, on the other hand, let us see into the inner workings of the MC's craft through the lyrical artifact of its creation.

The MC's most basic challenge is this: When given a beat, what do you do? The beat is rap's beginning. Whether it's the hiccups and burps of a Timbaland track, the percussive assault of a Just Blaze beat, knuckles knocking on a lunchroom table, a human beatbox, or simply the metronomic rhythm in an MC's head as he spits a cappella rhymes, the beat defines the limits of lyrical possibility. In transcribing rap lyrics, we must have a way of representing the beat on the page.

The vast majority of rap beats are in 4/4 time, which means that each musical measure (or bar) comprises four quarter-note beats. For the rapper, one beat in a bar is akin to the literary poet's metrical foot. Just as the fifth metrical foot marks the end of a pentameter line, the fourth beat of a given bar marks the end of the MC's line. One line, in other words, is what an MC can deliver in a single musical measure—one poetic line equals one musical bar. So when an MC spits sixteen bars, we should understand this as sixteen lines of rap verse.

To demonstrate this method of lyrical transcription, let's take a fairly straightforward example: Melle Mel's first verse on Grandmaster Flash and the Furious Five's classic "The Message."

One   **TWO**   **Three**   **FOUR**
Standing on the front stoop, hangin' out the window,
watching all the cars go by, roaring as the breezes blow.

Notice how the naturally emphasized words ("standing," "front," "hangin'," "window," etc.) fall on the strong beats. These are two fairly regular lines, hence the near uniformity of the pair and the strong-beat accents on particular words. The words are in lockstep with the beat. Mark the beginning of each poetic line on the one and the end of the line on the four.

Not all lines, however, are so easily transcribed; many complications can occur in the process of transcription. Consider the famous opening lines from this very same song:

One   **TWO**   **Three**   **FOUR**
Broken glass everywhere,
people pissin' on the stairs, you know they just don't care.

Looking at the two lines on the page, one might think that they had been incorrectly transcribed. The only thing that suggests they belong together is the end rhyme ("everywhere" and "care"). How can each of these lines—the first half as long as the second, and with fewer than half the total syllables—take up the same four-beat measure? The answer has everything to do with performance. Melle Mel delivers the first line with a combination of dramatic pause and exaggerated emphasis. He begins rhyming a little behind the beat, includes a caesura (a strong phrasal pause within the line) between "glass" and "everywhere," and then dramatically extenuates the pronunciation of "everywhere." Were it not for an accurate transcription, these poetic effects would be lost.

Sometimes rap poets devise intricate structures that give logical shape to their creations. Using patterns of rhyme, rhythm, and line, these structures reinforce an individual verse's fusion of form and meaning. While literary poetry often follows highly regularized forms—a sonnet, a villanelle, a ballad stanza—rap is rarely so formally explicit, favoring instead those structures drawn naturally from oral expression. Upon occasion, however, rap takes on more formal structures, either by happenstance or by conscious design. For instance, Long Beach's Crooked I begins the second verse of "What That Mean" by inserting an alternating quatrain, switching up the song's established pattern of rhyming consecutive lines.

> Shorty saw him comin' in a glare
> I pass by like a giant blur
> What she really saw was Tim Duncan in the air
> Wasn't nothin' but a Flyin' Spur

By rhyming two pairs of perfect rhymes *abab* ("glare" with "air" and "blur" with "spur"), Crooked I fashions a duality of sound that underscores the two perspectives he describes: that of the woman onlooker and that of the MC in his speeding car. By temporarily denying the listener's expectation of rhyme, he creates a sense of heightened anticipation and increased attention. Using this new rhyme pattern shines a spotlight on the playful metaphor at the center of the verse: what the woman saw was the San Antonio Spurs' MVP Tim Duncan in the air, otherwise known as a flying Spur, otherwise known as his luxury automobile, a Bentley Continental Flying Spur. The mental process of deciphering the metaphor, nearly instantaneous for those familiar with the reference and likely indecipherable for anyone else, is facilitated by the rhyming structure of the verse. Rhyme and wordplay work together to create a sense of poetic satisfaction.

Rap's poetry is best exemplified in these small moments that reveal conscious artistry at work in places we might least expect. It is this sense of craft that connects the best poetry of the past with the best rap of today. Consider the following two verses side by side: on the left is Langston Hughes's "Sylvester's Dying Bed," written in 1931; on the right is a transcription of Ice-T's "6 'N the Mornin'," released in 1987. Though distanced by time, these lyrics are joined by form.

Hughes's form relies upon splitting the conventional four-beat line in half, a pattern I have followed with Ice-T's verse for the purposes of comparison; I might just as easily have rewritten Hughes's lines as two sets of rhyming couplets. This adjustment aside, the two lyrics are nearly identical in form. Each employs a two-beat line (or a four-beat line cut in two) with an *abcb* rhyme pattern. They even share the same syntactical units, with *end stops* (a grammatical pause for punctuation at the end of a line of verse) on lines two, four, six, and eight. Both draw upon the rhythms of the vernacular, the language as actually spoken. This formal echo, reaching across more than a half century of black poetic expression, suggests a natural affinity of forms.

I woke up this mornin'	Six in the mornin'
'Bout half past three.	Police at my door.
All the womens in town	Fresh Adidas squeak
Was gathered round me.	Across my bathroom floor.
Sweet gals was a-moanin',	Out my back window,
"Sylvester's gonna die!"	I made my escape.
And a hundred pretty mamas	Don't even get a chance
Bowed their heads to cry.	To grab my old school tape.

Rap lyrics properly transcribed reveal themselves in ways not possible when listening to rap alone. Seeing rap on the page, we understand it for what it is: a small machine of words. We distinguish end rhymes from internal rhymes, end-stopped lines from enjambed ones, patterns from disruptions. Of course, nothing can replace the listening experience, whether in your headphones or at a show. Rather than replacing the music, reading rap as poetry heightens both enjoyment and understanding. Looking at rhymes on the page slows things down, allowing listeners—now readers—to discover familiar rhymes as if for the first time.

Walt Whitman once proclaimed that "great poets need great audiences." For over thirty years, rap has produced more than its share of great poets. Now it is our turn to become a great audience, repaying their efforts with the kind of close attention to language that rap's poetry deserves.

Part One

ONE Rhythm

RHYTHM IS RAP'S reason for being. I realized this several years ago in an unlikely place, a beach in a small seaside town outside of Rio de Janeiro. Unable to speak Portuguese, I had been making do by resorting to the traveler's Esperanto of smiles and hand gestures, but I hungered for familiar words. One afternoon as I walked along the beach, I contented myself by idly reciting rap verses that came to mind. I was in the midst of Inspectah Deck's opening lines from the Wu-Tang Clan's "Triumph" ("I bomb atomically, Socrates' philosophies / and hypotheses can't define how I be dropping these / mockeries") when I heard the first words uttered by another person that I had clearly understood in days.

"Wu-Tang Clan!"

I glanced behind me, half expecting to see some spectral projection of my linguistically isolated mind. Instead I saw a brown-skinned kid of about fourteen who seemed to have emerged from out of nowhere on the otherwise-abandoned beach. Not wanting to miss the chance to converse with someone in English, I asked him which MCs he liked best. He smiled broadly but said nothing. He'd exhausted his English, as I had my Portuguese. We parted ways, but I wondered, *What was it about those rhymes that spoke to him when the words could not?* It must have been the rhythm.

Rhythm is rap's basic element. Whatever else it is, rap is patterned verbal expression. It is the offspring of a voice and a beat. The beat, of course, is the most obvious rhythm we hear. It is the kick drum, the high hat, the snare. It is sampled or digitized, beatboxed, or even tapped out on a tabletop. The MC's voice has rhythm as well, playing off and on the beat in antagonistic cooperation. For most rap listeners, even for those with a full grasp of the language of the lyrics, rhythm has a way of overshadowing meaning. Feminist women sometimes hit the dance floor when the rhythm is right, misogynist lyrics be damned. And even true hip-hop heads have been known to "walk it out" or crank that Soulja Boy on occasion. The rhythm can make you do strange things. Rap, after all, is more than the sum of its sense; rhythm has a meaning all its own.

So what does rap mean when we aren't paying close attention or can't comprehend the words? "I can go to Japan, not speak the language or communicate whatsoever, but a beat will come on, and we'll all move our heads the same way," remarks Evidence of Dilated Peoples. "It lets me know that there's something bigger than just making rap songs." Less obvious but equally significant is that rap's poetic language also finds meaning in pure rhythmic expression. "Poetic forms are like that," literary critic Paul Fussell explains. "They tend to say things even if words are not at the moment fitted to their patterns."

Poetry was born in rhythm rather than in words. The first poem might well have been a cry uttered by one of our ancient ancestors long before modern language emerged. As poet and critic Robert Penn Warren once noted, from a groan to a sonnet is a straight line. In its simplest terms, then, a poem is a reproduction of the living tones of speech, regardless of meaning.

When the great Irish poet W. B. Yeats observed that poetry is "an elaboration of the rhythms of common speech and their association with profound feeling," he understood what I had only begun to comprehend on that beach in Brazil. Part of rap's appeal comes from its proximity to conversation; the rest lies in its necessary distance. Rap insists upon being understood. At least for those initiated into the culture, rap talks directly to us in a language we understand. But even plainspoken MCs—perhaps especially them, because they flow so low to the ground—rely upon those essential qualities that elevate rap beyond everyday expression. No matter how conversational an MC's lyrics may sound, their rhythm makes them poetry.

Rap is what results when MCs take the natural rhythms of everyday speech and reshape them to a beat. The drumbeat is rap's heartbeat; its metronomic regularity gives rap its driving energy and inspires the lyricist's creativity. "Music only needs a pulse," the RZA of the Wu-Tang Clan explains.

"Even a hum, with a bass and snare—it'll force a pulse, a beat. It makes order out of noise." Robert Frost put it even more plainly: "The beat of the heart seems to be basic in all making of poetry in all languages." In rap, whether delivered in English or Portuguese, Korean or Farsi, we hear two and sometimes many more rhythms layered on top of one another. The central rhythmic relationship, though, is always between the beat and the voice. As the RZA explains, the beat should "inspire that feeling in an MC, that spark that makes him want to grab a mic and rip it."

Rappers have a word for what they do when the rhythm sparks them; they call it *flow*. Simply put, flow is an MC's distinctive lyrical cadence, usually in relation to a beat. It is rhythm over time. In a compelling twist of etymology, the word *rhythm* is derived from the Greek *rheo*, meaning "flow." Flow is where poetry and music communicate in a common language of rhythm. It relies on tempo, timing, and the constitutive elements of *linguistic prosody*: accent, pitch, timbre, and intonation.

Like jazz musicians, MCs boast about staying in the pocket of the beat, finding the place where their voices are rhythmically in sync with the drums. When Kanye West raps on "Get 'Em High" that "my rhyme's in the pocket like wallets / I got the bounce like hydraulics," he is bragging about his flow. An effective rap lyricist must satisfy the listener's innate desire for order by rapping, for the most part, in the pocket. This doesn't mean simply flowing in lockstep with the track at all times; that can sound dull after only a few bars. Instead, a talented MC creates moments of calculated rhythmic surprise. Good rappers combine the expected metrical scheme with altered or exaggerated speech intonations to create a distinctive sense of rhythm, a flow all their own. They know when to switch up their flows to fit a new beat or a new lyrical mood. They know how to deliver variety without violating the integrity of the rhythm.

Part of the synergy of beats and rhymes is that they protect each other from their own potential excesses. Beats without voices soon become monotonous. Rhymes in isolation expose the frailty of the human voice and the fallibility of the rapper's vocal rhythms. Together, however, beats and rhymes find strength: The voice gives the beat humanity and variety; the beat gives the rhyme a reason for being and a margin for error. This essential relationship is rap's greatest contribution to the rhythm of poetry: the *dual rhythmic relationship*.

Rap's dual rhythmic relationship liberates the MC to pursue innovations of syncopation and stress that might otherwise sound chaotic were it not for the reassuring regularity of the beat. The beat and the MC's flow work together to satisfy the audience's musical and poetic expectations of rhythm: that it establish and maintain distinct patterns while creatively disrupting those patterns, through syncopation and other pleasing forms of rhythmic surprise. The rapper Q-Tip remembers the moment when he first realized this dual rhythmic relationship for himself. "Well, initially, [I would] probably just [write] my rhymes, spitting over the beat and making it fit," he recalls. "Then I realized that my voice was an instrument, and, slowly but surely, I started to get into rhythms, cadences, and becoming another instrument along with what was already there." When beats and rhymes work together, they achieve an organic unity of rhythm that is more powerful than most literary verses can likely achieve.

To hear lyrics set to the beat for which they were written is to experience an epiphany of sound.

Rap is poetry's greatest throwback to rhythm. Even new-school rap is old-school poetry. At the same time, rap has advanced the metrical tradition in startling ways by crafting a dual rhythmic voice that both maintains an old-school allegiance to meter even as it engages in a new-school exploration of rhythm. This does not mean that MCs write their lyrics in iambic pentameter and trochaic trimeter; rap's lyrical relation to poetic meter is more informal and improvisational than that. Rather, rap's meter is the drumbeat and its rhythm is the MC's flow on top of the beat.

Among the many things that distinguish hip-hop lyricism from literary poetry, rap's dual rhythmic voice is the most essential. Rap makes audible a rhythmic relationship that is only theoretical in conventional verse. In literary poetry, the difference between meter and rhythm is the difference between the ideal and the actual rhythms of a given poetic line. *Poetic meter*, in other words, is structured rhythm; it defines the ideal pattern of a given sequence of stressed and unstressed (also known as accented and unaccented) syllables. To quote Paul Fussell, meter is "what results when the natural rhythmical movements of colloquial speech are heightened, organized, and regulated so that pattern—which means repetition—emerges from the relative phonetic haphazard of ordinary utterance."

Poetic rhythm, on the other hand, is the natural pattern of speech in relation to a given meter. Along with rhyme, it is the music of words. Where meter is ideal, rhythm is real. In poetry the only rhythm that is "audible," either in the reader's head or in the speaker's voice reciting the poem, is the imperfect rhythm, not the perfect meter. A literary poet creates variety by working with and against a silent and implicit metrical perfection. Stray too far from the meter and the poem can lose all rhythmic order, stay too close and it begins to sound like a singsong parody of itself.

Scansion is the technique by which we identify a poem's meter by marking the stresses (or accents) and determining the overall rhythm pattern of the verse. A stress is nothing more than the vocal emphasis naturally given to a particular syllable when spoken compared to the emphasis given to those around it. Anything written can be scanned, from an individual multisyllabic word to the sentence you are reading now. Scansion is most useful, however, when the poet has patterned his or her language to follow an established metrical order of accented and unaccented syllables organized into repeating units, or *feet*.

Scanning a poem often requires as much art as science, because we must read the verse with possible metrical patterns in mind, but also with an overall sense of the natural rhythms at work in the lines. To take an obvious example, we identify the meter of Shakespeare's sonnet 18 ("Shall *I* com*pare* thee *to* a *sum*mer's *day*? / Thou *art* more *love*ly *and* more *tem*per*ate*") as iambic pentameter not because it is perfectly composed of five sets of unstressed syllables followed by stressed syllables per line but because the verse as a whole *approaches* this ideal. Even Shakespeare—especially Shakespeare—wrote lines with irregular scansion, both out of measured poetic effect and the inevitable rhythmic imprecision of the English language itself. Shakespeare's rhythm is born of the creative tension between an established metrical pattern and its natural intonation when spoken by a human voice. He fashioned a rhythm that is both recognizable as iambic pentameter and distinguishable enough from that metrical ideal to give his sonnet a human voice.

Historically, Western poetry has favored such regular metrics. However, contemporary verse has shifted decidedly toward less-predictable accentual rhythm patterns. "Today," writes poet Timothy Steele, "one almost hesitates to say that most poets write unmetrically; such a statement suggests that they know what meter is, which does not appear to be the case. Rather, it seems that versification, as it has been understood for millennia, is for the majority of contemporary poets an irrelevant matter." This may be putting it a bit too strongly; many free-verse poets are still concerned with rhythm, creating smaller rhythmic motifs in their verse. But by rejecting regular metrical patterns and often rhyme as well, literary poetry has lost a good share of its popular appeal.

If you ask most people to describe a poem, they'll tell you that it rhymes and that it has discernable rhythm. That so many modern literary poets have chosen not to fulfill these expectations in favor of experimenting with a broader range of formal possibilities undoubtedly accounts for some of literary poetry's greatest innovations in craft but also for its decline as a popular medium in our time.

Understanding accentual meter means understanding how sounds join together to make sense. English, more than most other languages, relies on stressed syllables to convey meaning. Linguists recognize four or even more different weights that syllables can carry in English, and true adherents to metrical analysis have devised any number of notations to account for the subtle valences of stress in a given line of verse. For our purposes, however, it is most useful to distinguish between syllables that an MC accords significant stress and those delivered with less inflection. As a general rule, the more significant the word (or part of a word), the more stress it receives. Of course no two people will read the same sentence in exactly the same way. Any arrangement of words embodies a range of potential accentual interpretations that can change depending on anything from tone to the speaker's accent to his or her emotion. The heightened prominence of one syllable in relation to others can be rendered by any number of means, from volume to pitch to length of stress. Depending on the meaning the speaker wishes to convey, stress alone can make a world of difference.

Patterns of accent form the ground upon which rap's poetry and music meet in shared sound. It is particularly fitting that the word *accent* derives from the Latin term *accentus*, which means "song added to speech," for it is precisely the arrangement of accents that gives language its music. For rap lyricists, then, the stresses they put on syllables are the means by which they arrange the music of the human voice. This is another definition of flow: the song the rapper's speech sings. Take these lines from a rap song even people who hate rap probably know: "Now, this is a story all about how / My life got flipped, turned upside down." Without hearing the track or Will Smith's (aka the Fresh Prince's) flow, we can already glean a wealth of rhythmic information from the words themselves and their arrangement across the lines. We hear the *enjambment* (or break in the syntactic unit) between "how" and "my"; we note the unresolved tension of the slant rhyme ("how" and "down") as it plays itself out in the rhythm. Reading alone, however, has its limitations. If we wish to understand rhythm in rap's poetry, we must begin with the beat.

Beat is something we talk about in both rap and literary verse, but in strikingly different ways. Chuck D breaks it down like this: "Poetry makes the beat come to *it*, and rap pretty much is subservient to the beat." This subservience, of course, is not absolute, yet even the most rhythmically daring MCs—Busta Rhymes, Ol' Dirty Bastard, E-40—pledge allegiance to the beat. Unlike the rhythms of literary poetry, then, the rhythms of rap are governed by something outside of the MC's own literary conceptions. Rap's beat serves an analogous purpose for the MC that meter does for the literary poet: Namely, it sets out the terms of a rhythmic ideal. One might even consider hip hop's beat as poetic meter rendered audible, clarifying the relationship between metrical perfection and rhythmic innovation.

Rap flaunts its metric perfection even as it allows for rhythmic invention. The beat's integrity, however, is not absolute. While hip hop usually employs 4/4 time—meaning that it has four beats per measure—not every measure is composed of quarter notes. Measures can consist of eighth notes, sixteenth notes, half notes, whole notes, held notes, etc. Though drum machines and digital sequencing make it possible to achieve superhuman perfection, most producers embrace the slight flaws found in sampled live instrumental performance. Rhythmic variety, therefore, exists even in the beat itself. Still, the beat's relative predictability compared to human voice clears a space for the MC to stray from expectation even as the overall performance satisfies it. Rap has succeeded where most contemporary literary poetry has not; it has retained its popular appeal for predictability while still liberating the MC to explore the formal possibilities of rhythm.

The story of rap's dual rhythmic revolution begins, as so many stories do in hip hop, with two turntables and a microphone. In the mid-1970s, New York DJs looking for new ways to rock the party started improvising chants in between songs. Sometimes they would loop the hottest part of the record, capturing a drum sequence called a break, then talk over that. They would shout out their own names or the name of their crews, they would tell the crowds what to do— it didn't really matter, as long as they said something over the break. Audiences couldn't get enough.

DJ Kool Herc was one of the first to do it. He had emigrated with his family from Jamaica to the South Bronx in 1967, bringing with him the sound of his native island and a love of American soul music. By the mid-seventies he began throwing neighborhood block parties with his massive sound system banging out percussive funk, soul, and reggae. "Just to hear the bass was like everything," Sha-Rock, one of the earliest female MCs, recalls. "To hear the bass. You know? . . . The music. James Brown . . . all these different types of music that you could breakdance to. Herc, he'll get on there and say like one or two words. . . . Herc wasn't like a rapper or anything like that; it was just a sound, his music, his system. The music that he played was like no other." Soon rapping would develop into something more, as the rhymes started to emerge on their own as distinct from, yet still on, the beat. This was the birth of the MC.

The DJ spun the records and the MC played a supporting role as master of ceremonies, offering up a chant or a few lyrical lines to punctuate the music. The rhymes were often as basic as hip-hop pioneer DJ Hollywood's signature call: "Hollywood, I'm doing good, and I hope you're feeling fine." All it took were words rhyming in rhythm. In rap's early years the lyrics often read like nursery rhymes. This is no disrespect to hip hop's pioneers. Rather, it is a testament to the way that rap tapped into that most basic human need for rhythm that poetry was created to satisfy.

Melvin "Melle Mel" Glover, whom many regard as the father of the modern MC, was only a teenager when he partnered with two other rappers—his brother Nathaniel Glover, aka Kid Creole, and Keith Wiggins, aka Cowboy—and joined with the now legendary DJ Grandmaster Flash (Joseph Saddler). Together, they built on Herc's model. "The Kool Herc style at the time was basically freelance talking," Grandmaster Flash explains, "not necessarily syncopated to the beat. The three of them—Cowboy, Creole, and Mel—came up with this style called the back and forth, where they would be MC-ing to the beat that I would play. I'll take a sentence that hopefully the whole world knows: 'Eeeny, meeny, miny mo, catch a piggy by the toe.' So they devised it where Cowboy might say 'Eeeny meeny,' and then Creole would say, 'Miny,' and then Mel would say, 'Mo.' So they would kind of bounce it around." The essential difference between a DJ motivating the crowd on the mic and an MC rapping to a beat was twofold: syncopation and sound, rhythm and rhyme.

Rap as we know it was born only after words started bending to the beat. It was founded on that dual rhythmic relationship. Those who trace rap back to earlier forms of black oral expression often overlook this distinguishing difference. Though folk practices like the dozens (a game of ritual insult) and the toasts (long narrative poems, often with explicit subject matter) resemble modern-day rap in the way they play with words, they lack the fundamental dual rhythmic relationship that characterizes rap. For all Muhammad Ali's brilliant rhyme and wordplay, he never said his lines over a beat. For all their smoothed-out love patter, soul crooners like Barry White did it as singers rather than as rhymers. Rap's most striking contribution to the black American oral tradition—indeed, to American culture as a whole—is this rhythmic sophistication, rap's outward manifestation of the meter and rhythm of literary verse.

Considering rap's development from its early years to its golden age, Marcus Reeves keenly observes that "MCs were elevating the art of rhyme, utilizing the layered intricacy of sampled rhythms to enhance the meter of their poetry, approaching the delivery of their words like musicians and poets. With labyrinthine flows and off-rhyming techniques, this new breed of MC laced his/her lyrics with complex wordplay, titillating the ear and imagination of listeners much the way bebop pioneers intensified the riffs, solos, and chord changes of their swinging forefathers." As both musicians and poets, rappers faced the boon and the burden of fitting language to the shape of their lyrical impulses and their grandest conceptions.

While the recordings of rap's earliest innovators seem simplistic when set beside a verse from Talib Kweli or Immortal Technique, those earlier artists had to invent the basic rules of the form even as they wrote their rhymes. "Every subsequent generation of MCs had a whole genealogy of artists to define themselves against," historian William Jelani Cobb explains. "Melle Mel had a pen, a pad and an idea." Great art is defined by both invention and refinement. Rap's early hits show hip-hop poetry in the process of invention, still defining its form even as it kept moving the crowd. A good place to observe this process is in rap's first crossover hit, the Sugar Hill Gang's "Rapper's Delight."

For anyone listening to music in 1979, at least for anyone outside of New York City, it is almost certain that the first rap song they ever heard was the Sugar Hill Gang's "Rapper's Delight." For anyone born later on—ten or more years after the song first appeared—at least some of its lyrics will be familiar. "I said a-hip hop, the-hippy / the-hippy to the hip hip-hop you don't stop!" Most people are aware that "Rapper's Delight" was rap's first mainstream radio hit. Some are aware of its controversial history—how Sylvia Robinson, the founder of Sugar Hill Records, assembled a group of pizza-delivery boys and bouncers to record the song; how most of the lyrics were allegedly stolen from the true MCs who wrote them; how the song does not reflect the authentic spirit of rap as defined by the people who were creating it at that very moment. And while all of this is a vital part of the song's history, it does not erase the indisputable truth that "Rapper's Delight" marks a kind of beginning for rap in the public imagination. The 12-inch version of "Rapper's Delight" was nearly fifteen minutes long, an eternity when most radio-ready singles were clocking in at under four minutes. In spite of this, the song climbed the charts in the fall of 1979, reaching #4 on the R&B charts and even cracking the top 40 (at #36) on the disco-dominated pop charts.

The first noticeable thing about the song isn't the rap at all, but the bass line—an unmistakable riff lifted from Chic's disco hit of that same year, "Good Times." The second is the drums, a wicked kick and a snare accented by hand claps. It is clear that this is a party anthem even before the rappers grab the mic. When Wonder Mike comes in, rhyming that unmistakable bit of hip-hop gibberish, whoever was listening could immediately hear that rap was something new. Here were voices that were not singing, not speaking, but somehow doing a little of both at the same time. For a generation of listeners, this was the rebirth of cool.

In a striking 2006 article for the *Washington Post* entitled "Why I Gave Up on Hip-Hop," Lonnae O'Neal Parker recalls her own conflicted relationship with the music—a relationship that began when she fell in love with "Rapper's Delight." It was more than a song, she explains; for her, and other young black kids like her, it helped shape both her sense of art and her sense of self. "I was 12," she recalls, "the same age my oldest daughter is now, when hip-hop began to shape my politics and perceptions and aesthetics. It gave me a meter for my thoughts and bent my mind toward metaphor and rhyme. I couldn't sing a lick, but didn't hip-hop give me the beginnings of a voice."

The beginnings of a voice, a distinctly black voice, reveal the essential confluence of politics and poetics in rap. Granted, "Rapper's Delight" is an unlikely political anthem, and certainly it is as far removed as you can imagine from the social critique of a later recording like Grandmaster Flash and the Furious Five's "The Message," and yet despite its particular subject matter, it embodied a radical political sensibility in the sheer exuberance and spirit of its voices. The very act of expression, even in the admittedly flawed and conflicted reality of the song's origins, even in the seeming vacuity of its good-times subject matter, marks a kind of revolution in black aesthetics.

It also marked a surprising poetic development as well. "Rapper's Delight" stands as an example of rap at its most basic. Its rhymes always fall at the end of lines. Its rhythms are almost completely dominated by the beat rather than the

MC's distinctive flow. To ears accustomed to the verbal acro-batics of Eminem or the understated complexity of Jay-Z, these lyrics seem almost embarrassingly rudimentary. But even here, with rap at its most basic, subtle poetics are in practice. Rap's revolution in poetic rhythm has already begun.

The poetic revolution in "Rapper's Delight" is rooted, oddly enough, in the old poetic tradition of the ballad. Ballad meter, also called common measure, dates from at least as early as the thirteenth century, when the oldest extant ballad, *Judas*, was recorded in manuscript form. Ballad form fits the structure of song, lending itself to memorization and musical performance. With some variation, it has emerged through the centuries more or less intact in the form of four-line stanzas or quatrains consisting alternately of four and three stresses apiece, rhyming *abcb* (and occasionally *abab*). The rhythm achieved by the ballad stanza is immediately recognizable even when left unidentified. It is one of the ba-sic rhythms of our culture.

> Now **WHAT** you **HEAR** is **NOT** a **TEST**
> I'm **RAP**pin' **TO** the **BEAT**.
> And **ME**, the **GROOVE**, **AND** my **FRIENDS**
> are gonna **TRY** to **MOVE** your **FEET**.

Wonder Mike need not have set out to deliver his rhyme in ballad stanzas, he need only to have come of age in a cul-ture where, regardless of race, class, or circumstance, he would be exposed to the rhythms and rhymes of this elemen-tal form. Whether through an advertising jingle or a gospel hymn, a television theme or a classic literary verse, the bal-lad form asserts itself upon the consciousness of all around it, regardless of race, class, or any other distinction.

Wonder Mike's likely unwitting use of ballad stanzas underscores two essential facts about rap poetics. Rap was created by black Americans. Rap is a Western poetic form. These are not contradictory assertions. "Blacks alone didn't invent poetics any more than they invented the American language," Ralph Ellison once argued when asked about the "black aesthetic." "And the necessary mixture of cultural influences that goes into creating an individual poetic style defies the neat over-simplifications of racist ideologies." The revolutionary nature of rap, in these early days all the way to the present, lies in the constant defiance of racist assumptions about the cultural fluency of black artists. The caricature of the artistically and intellectually impoverished street thug so often put forward by critics of so-called gangsta rap fails to account for the linguistic virtuosity and cultural literacy required to rap effectively to a beat.

It is no mere coincidence, then, that rap lyrics respond so well to the classical tools of poetic analysis. The opening lines of "Rapper's Delight" approximate the meter of the iambic foot, an unstressed syllable followed by a stressed one. The first two lines of the verse follow strict iambic meter, and the third line seems to be doing the same until something happens in the middle—two stressed syllables in a row ("groove and"). Further complicating matters, the next line begins with three unstressed syllables in a row ("are gonna") before returning to a regular iambic meter. These irregularities do not signal a flaw in the rhyme, nor do they suggest an error in our method of analysis. Rather, they prove the point that rap's rhythm is not governed by strict metrics alone but by the beat of the drums and the individual creativity of the lyricist.

If we now go back and listen to the track, we'll notice a couple important things. First, Wonder Mike is rapping securely in the pocket of the beat. Hand claps punctuate the twos and the fours, lending extra emphasis to the words he stresses; for instance, "hear" falls on the two and "test" falls on the four. Second, his flow actually gives the doubled-up stresses in the third line room to breath by including a slight pause between "groove" and "and" that the written words on the page do not suggest. Similarly, he lessens the effect of the three unstressed syllables by further truncating his pronunciation of "gonna." The resulting rhythm is unmistakably related to iambic meter, yet loose enough to sound unforced and natural.

Almost two centuries before "Rapper's Delight," Samuel Taylor Coleridge's *The Rime of the Ancient Mariner* employed the ballad form for many of the same reasons. He chose the form for its musicality, and also for its efficacy as a storytelling medium. The poem's opening lines, like the opening lines of "Rapper's Delight," set the rhythm as well as the story.

> It is an Ancient Mariner,
> And he stoppeth one of three.
> By thy long grey beard and glittering eye,
> Now wherefore stopp'st thou me?

Beyond the similarity of form, *The Rime of the Ancient Mariner* and "Rapper's Delight" share a common purpose in storytelling. The ballad stanza harkens back to literary poetry's oral tradition when rhythm and rhyme served as mnemonic devices enabling the poet or speaker to recall long narrative passages. Perhaps the best-known example of the ballad stanza in pop culture is the theme from *Gilligan's Island*; for one of the least likely mash-ups in history try singing the tune using the Sugar Hill Gang or Coleridge's words. What the Sugar Hill Gang, Samuel Taylor Coleridge, and whoever wrote the "Gilligan's Island" theme understood—either explicitly or intuitively—was that the ballad form creates pleasing rhythms that approximate natural speech patterns in English, helping to tell a story.

"Rapper's Delight" was at once new to the music world, but true to the poetic tradition. It's a safe guess, however, that Wonder Mike was not counting the number of stresses in his lines, nor was he consciously modeling his verse on the ballad stanza. What the formal resemblance reminds us is that poetic form grows out of the natural habits of speech. When poets understand those forms, they are able to control with greater accuracy the effects those forms will have on their audience. When an audience understands the forms, they are better prepared to respond with sensitivity and awareness to the poet's creations.

With the thirty-year anniversary of "Rapper's Delight," it is instructive to reflect upon what remains of its once-startling appeal. When played today, it has a quaint and kitschy sort of funkiness, more akin to the disco records of the era than the radical rejection of disco that rap amounted to at the time. The rhymes sound naïve to those acquainted with the street themes of Rick Ross and Young Jeezy and the intricate poetics of Nas and Ghostface. And those who know the song's history can't help but hear it as a fraud perpetrated on the unschooled ears of the masses. Even the rhymes themselves are flawed; they are too insistently dictated by the rhythm of the track. They fall into or, rather, helped to fashion the singsongy style that dominates many old-school rhymes. It was a necessary precursor to today's rap poetics, and yet it is as distinct from contemporary rap as Mother Goose is from Wallace Stevens. And yet for all of this, "Rapper's Delight" is a landmark recording in rap's poetic tradition: It makes beauty out of little more than rhythm alone.

Rap's early years are rich with easily observable poetic forms like those of "Rapper's Delight." The sound that would soon come to be identified as "old school" is a product of MCs' strict reliance on formal patterns like the ballad stanza. Listen to these lines from the Fatback Band's 1979 "King Tim III (Personality Jock)," widely considered to be the first rap ever released, and you hear echoes of "Row, Row, Row Your Boat," given subversive new lyrics:

> Roll, roll, roll your joint
> Twist it at the ends
> You light it up, you take a puff
> And then you pass it to your friends.

Or listen to Run-DMC's alliterative take on Peter Piper:

> Peter Piper picked peppers,
> But Run rock rhymes.

Nursery rhymes have long been a source of inspiration for poets of all kinds. Robert Frost once described the childhood source of poetic rhythm like this: "You may not realize it," he writes, "but it is the way you have all come thus far from the days of your Godmother Goose through books and nature, gathering bits and scraps of real magic that however flowery still clung to you like burrs thrown on your clothes in holiday foolery. You don't have to worry about clinging to such trophies. They will cling to you." Poetic rhythms cling to us from our earliest childhood memories, and like magic we can tap into these formative lyrical experiences throughout our lifetimes. That rap understands this lyrical magic so well helps explain its longevity.

While all poetry has its roots in our childhood love of rhyme, this relation is often most visible at the birth of a new poetic movement. This was certainly the case with hip hop, which seemed in its early years to revel in its naughty sendups of childhood verse that celebrated the familiar rhythms of common verse. As the years went by and rap developed a poetic heritage all its own, the general trend moved away from the rudimentary roots of rap's early rhythms and rhymes to a more nuanced poetics. And yet rather than look down upon those early rhymes as rudimentary or restrictive, we might remember them as the necessary and revolutionary poetic acts that they were: bending the most rigid forms of an inherited tradition to a new purpose—new voices, new sounds, new ways of describing the world and the people in it.

When tracing rap's poetic roots, one is naturally drawn to the oral tradition. Oral poetry, from the lyric to the epic, has deep roots in most every continent, certainly in West Africa where the poet functioned as much as a musician as a wordsmith, weaving narrative verse around patterns of call-and-response with an active audience. For many rappers and scholars, rap's connection to African poetic practice, charged as it is with symbolic meaning, is the most important progenitor to the poetics of contemporary rap. KRS-One makes the connection between rappers and griots, as much for their function within the community as for their aesthetic methods. This remains an essential bond, one with vital importance for the black diasporic tradition.

As a practical matter of poetics, however, rap is most directly connected to the Western poetic tradition of the ballad and other metrical forms. To say that rap takes its form from Western sources is not, however, to whitewash its identity. Since its birth, rap has been a defiantly black form. Just as the early jazz musicians commandeered European marching band instruments like the saxophone and the trumpet and bent their sounds to fit the demands of a new expression, so, too, have African-American rap artists transformed the very poetic forms they've inherited. This is no less a creative act than if they had conceived the forms *sui generis*; indeed, it is the hallmark of a typically American, and specifically black American cultural practice, the vernacular process. Rap is a vernacular art, which is to say that it is born out of the creative combination of the inherited and the invented, the borrowed and the made.

One can hear in rap the Anglo-Saxon tradition of accentual or strong-stress meter in which each line contains the same number of natural speech stresses. The most common iteration includes four stressed syllables per line with each line divided in half by a medial caesura, or an extended pause. As the basis for everything from *Beowulf* to Mother Goose nursery rhymes, accentual meter is perhaps the most familiar poetic form around. It creates a stylized structure that is at once natural and yet immediately distinct from everyday speech.

The four-stress line has dominated popular verse from the Middle Ages to the present day in part because of its in-

herent orality. It promises enough regularity while still allowing for variability and surprise. In accentual meter only the
stressed syllables count; a line may have as many unstressed
syllables as it likes without compromising the form. Consider
the following example of four-stress accentual verse from a
common nursery rhyme:

> There **WAS** an old **WOMAN** who **LIVED** in a **SHOE**,
> She **HAD** so many **CHIL**dren, she didn't **KNOW** what to **DO**;
> She **GAVE** them some **BROTH** with**OUT** any **BREAD**,
> She **WHIPPED** them all **SOUNDLY**, and **PUT** them to **BED**.

While each of the lines has four strongly stressed syllables,
the total number of syllables differs significantly: Line two has
fourteen syllables, while line three has only ten. The result is
a rhyme with order as well as variety. MCs have made an art
out of exploiting the range of syllables in given lines. Bun B,
for instance, believes that a rapper's virtuosity is at least partly
a product of the artful manipulation of syllables. When asked
how he might go about outrapping another MC, he explains
it in terms of syllables. "If he uses ten syllables in a line, I'm
going to use fifteen," he said. "If he uses fifteen, I'm going to
use twenty, twenty-five." And yet often these hypersyllabic
lines still include only four strongly stressed syllables.

Rap veteran Busta Rhymes has developed a style that
relies heavily upon both strong accents on unexpected
syllables and expansion and contraction of syllable count.
Among his most virtuosic performances is "Gimme Some
More," in which he delivers a rapid-fire sequence of syllables
underscored by assonance, alliteration, and other forms of
repetition.

> **FLASH** with a **RASH** gimme my **CASH** flickin' my **ASH**
> **RUN**nin' with my **MON**ey, son, go **OUT** with a **BLAST**
> **DO** what you **WAN**na, niggas **CUT**tin' the **COR**ner
> You fuckin' **UP** the arti**CLE**, go ahead and **MEET** the re**POR**ter

Not surprisingly, Busta lends the greatest emphasis to the most important words in each line: the words that rhyme ("flash," "rash," "cash," "ash," and the slant rhyme "blast") and the verbs ("runnin'," "meet"). The stressed words help constitute the rhythm of the line, defining the terms of Busta's flow. As the verse opens he establishes a clear pattern both of stress and syllable count; each of the first three lines contains twelve syllables. But the final line of the second couplet is dilated to contain sixteen syllables, a sonic feat that Busta achieves by accelerating the pace of his delivery.

Unless you are familiar with the lyrics and can replay Busta's performance in your head, you would be clueless in identifying most of the distinctive differences that define his flow, those qualities that set it apart from the conventional rhythms of everyday speech. Accentual stress, after all, is not the same as natural vocal inflection. One of the ways that an MC emphasizes his or her artistry is by bending words so that they fit into the MC's particular rhythm rather than adhere to the constraints of proper pronunciation. In Busta Rhymes's case we see a small example of this in the final line above, when he eschews the conventional pronunciation of "article," with the accent on the first syllable, for his newly wrought rendition of the word with the accent on the last syllable. The result is a small but significant transformation of sound, one that counts for rather little on its own but contributes mightily to the revolutionary effect of rap's poetics in action.

Big Daddy Kane is one of the truly revolutionary MCs in rap history when it comes to these matters of stress and articulation. He has expanded hip-hop poetics with his lyrical innovations, particularly when it comes to flow. Some of today's greatest lyricists—Nas, Jay-Z, Lil Wayne—count him among their primary influences. In classic rhymes like "Wrath of Kane," he experiments with vocal rhythms in ways that reward close analysis, not only of stress patterns, but of accentual-syllabic patterns as well. With his rapid-fire lines, laden with assonance, rich in rhyme—though often not in the expected place at the end of the line—he creates highly wrought, formal rhythmic structures.

> The **MAN** at **HAND** to **RULE** and **SCHOOL** and **TEACH**
> And **REACH** the **BLIND** to **FIND** their **WAY** from **A** to **Z**
> And **BE** the **MOST** and **BOAST** the **LOUD**est **RAP**
> **KANE'**ll **REIGN** your do**MAIN!** (Yeah, **KANE!**)

Three lines of iambs (a pentameter, a hexameter, and another pentameter) are boldly disrupted by a fourth trochaic line. In the lines following the four quoted above, he returns to a more loosely iambic rhythm, though not one that scans as neatly as the opening lines. The effect of the rhythm pattern Kane develops in these opening three lines is almost dizzying in its repetition, making it all the more effective when he breaks it off. Had the incessant iambs gone on undisrupted for another line or two, it would have begun to sound monotonous. Instead, Kane introduces just enough variation to keep his flow fresh and his audience entertained by the play of rhythmic satisfaction and surprise.

When that rhythmic expectation isn't satisfied, disaster usually follows. Rap without rhythm is an absurdity. There's a difference between rudimentary but functional rhythm and no rhythm at all. Because rap is an oral form, rhythmic errors are even more glaringly apparent. A wack flow is death to rap. Unfortunately, wack rhymes are everywhere, thanks to hip hop's rampant commercialization. Rap sells everything from cars to breakfast cereals. I'm not talking here about whatever you might hear on the radio or see in a music video; with the advent of computer technologies like Pro Tools, most every professional rapper can rhyme on beat—at least in the studio. I'm talking about the many raps you'll hear on TV commercials or on Saturday-morning cartoons. Worse still are those you'll read that weren't even written to be performed. Most such "raps" are either naïve attempts to dabble in youth culture or, worse, cynical efforts to scavenge from rap's "cool." One of the most glaring examples of the latter appeared on the Federal Emergency Management Agency's website at the time of Hurricane Katrina. It illustrates better than any recorded rap just what happens when rap loses its rhythm.

> Disaster . . . it can happen anywhere,
> But we've got a few tips, so you can be prepared
> For floods, tornadoes, or even a 'quake,
> You've got to be ready—so your heart don't break.
> Disaster prep is your responsibility
> And mitigation is important to our agency.
> People helping people is what we do
> And FEMA is there to help see you through
> When disaster strikes, we are at our best
> But we're ready all the time, 'cause disasters don't rest.

Putting aside the bitter irony of the lyrics, given FEMA's dreadful lack of preparation for disaster and failure to act in the aftermath of Katrina, the most noticeable thing about the verse is its rudimentary rhythm. You can see the writer—and this is undoubtedly a rhyme of the page, not of the voice—straining to establish his flow. The ellipses in the first line and the dash in the fourth are visual manifestations of rhythmic exhaustion. By isolating "disaster" from the rest of the first line he disrupts his flow even before it has a chance to begin. Part of the problem is that the writer has stranded each line from the ones that surround it, meaning that the rhythm screeches to halt no fewer than ten times in the ten-line verse. Notice the way the sixth line struggles to match the rhythm of the fifth by cramming in too many syllables. Rhythmic difficulties like this lead to forced rhymes (like "responsibility" and "our agency") or unimaginative ones (like "'quake" and "break"). With no rhythmic development, no flow at all, it bears no more than a surface relation to the rap it emulates.

Skilled MCs know the rhythmic weight of their words. Syllables can be light or heavy, long or short. An effective rap verse balances its linguistic weight in such a way that it can be performed without awkward pauses, gasps for breath, or other infelicities. Rap has made rhythm into a science, a point Paul D. Miller (better known as DJ Spooky) makes in his multimedia text, *Rhythm Science*. "Rhythm science," he explains, "is not so much a new language as a new way of pronouncing the ancient syntaxes that we inherit from history and evolution, a new way of enunciating the basic primal languages that slip through the fabric of rational thought and infect our psyche at another, deeper level." He is speaking here primarily about the language of sound on the level of music and the protolinguistic, but it undoubtedly relates to the lyrical side of rap's dual rhythmic relationship. "Give me two turntables," he boasts, "and I'll make you a universe." The right rap lyrics can do the same thing.

In the decades since "Rapper's Delight," and in the distance from unskilled attempts like the FEMA rap, hip hop has undergone a rhythmic revolution. Some of the best-known lyricists, from Nas to Talib Kweli, not to mention MCs in hip hop's thriving underground, have liberated their flows from the restrictions of rigid metrical patterns in favor of more expansive rhythmic vocabularies that include techniques like piling up stressed and unstressed syllables, playing against the beat, and altering normal pronunciation of words in favor of newly accented ones. We now live in a time when rap can mean any number of things, depending on the place of its origin, the style of its production, and the particular sensibility of its lyricist. Exploring rap rhythm today requires a close attention to the specific rhythmic innovations of individual artists.

Flow is an MC's lyrical fingerprint. We remember rap lyrics in their specific vocal contexts because of the MC's flow. Think of "99 Problems" and you'll distinctly hear Jay-Z's voice rhyming, "If you're havin' girl problems, I feel bad for you, son." Think of "Lose Yourself" and you'll hear Eminem's rapping, "Snap back to reality, oh, there goes gravity." No other voices could utter these words with the same style; imagining Eminem reciting Jay-Z's lines or visa versa just doesn't make sense. Pitch, intonation, accent, cadence, all flood our remembrance of the lyrics, setting the words in specific musical and poetic contexts. These contexts are not always coterminous—the musical concerns harmony and melody in instrumental accompaniment, the poetic concerns rhetorical figures and lyrical forms—but they overlap in their joint expression in rhythm.

It is here, in rhythm, that rap's relationship to lyric poetry most distinguishes itself from that of other pop music genres. This is not a distinction of kind, but rather of degree. Rock music and soul music and country and western music all, like rap, relate to poetry through rhythm. It is what music and poetry share in common. Poetry on the page has no melody or harmony; it is pure rhythm. Rap, though it frequently includes samples and choruses that employ memorable melodies and harmonies, expresses itself most powerfully in the dual rhythmic relationship between the beat of the drums and the flow of the voice.

MCs face a particular challenge, distinct from those faced by literary poets and song lyricists. Literary poets concern themselves with the rhythms in the language of their lines. They balance stressed syllables and select specific rhythm patterns to govern their compositions. They work with implied beats. The song lyricist, on the other hand, must contend with audible rhythms in addition to harmony and melody. Writing for a singing voice, they construct a melodic line that fits within the musical accompaniment. The MC's task embodies elements of both, combined with a particular set of concerns unique to rap. Unlike a literary poet, an MC's flow is not governed solely by the rhythmic structure of the poet's words, but by the audible rhythms of the track. Unlike song lyricists, MCs are concerned almost exclusively with rhythm. This specialization opens rap up to its most obvious criticism from musicians in other genres: Rap is not music, they say, because it doesn't care about harmony and melody. Rap, in other words, is nothing more than an extended drum solo, the rapper nothing more than another kick drum or snare.

This rhythmic preoccupation should not obscure the wide range of aesthetic decisions an MC has to make in every rhyme. When presented with a beat, the first question for the lyricist is this: How will you rhyme to it? Fast or slow? Monotone or animated? A little bit ahead, a little bit behind, or right in the pocket? The answer is as varied as the number of individuals willing to pick up the mic and spit. You'll notice that nowhere in these questions is, "What will you talk about?" Perhaps there are some MCs who begin this way; undoubtedly almost every MC has begun with that question at one time or another. But I would contend that the question of lyrical content almost always comes second to the more immediate concern of sound.

Like a jazz singer scatting to some big-band swing, the MC's most pressing lyrical challenge is in patterning sound rather than making meaning. If this were reversed, if a rapper's primary concern had to be sense before anything else, then it might likely lead to those good-intentioned efforts at conscious rap that cram political slogans into the rhymes with little concern for how it sounds. Very few listeners will have the patience for that. In rap you must convince people that they should hear you even before they know what you're saying. That doesn't mean that content can't be the most powerful part of a rhyme; often it is. But it is not the first thing to consider, and it's rarely the indispensable part.

The first thing a listener usually hears in rap is the MC's flow. Flow, as you'll recall, is the distinctive rhythm cadence a rapper's voice follows to a beat. It is rhythm over time. As historian William Jelani Cobb describes it, flow is "an individual time signature, the rapper's own idiosyncratic approach to the use of time." Controlling tempo, juxtaposing silence with sound, patterning words in clusters of syllables, all are ways of playing with rhythm over time. In addition to its use of time, flow also works by arranging stressed and unstressed syllables in interesting ways. In this regard, flow relates to meter in literary poetry in that both rely on the poet's artful manipulation of vocal emphasis. Just as classical composers score music, poets "score" words, using the embedded rhythms of vocal stress.

Every poem provides the reader with implicit instructions on how to read it. Give ten able readers a copy of Edgar Allan Poe's *Annabel Lee* and, except for variations of vocal tone and small matters of personal choice, the poem should sound just about the same in each instance. "It was many and many a year ago, / In a kingdom by the sea, / That a maiden there lived whom you may know / By the name of Annabel Lee." As long as the readers haven't willfully disregarded the rhythmic clues Poe has set down in his arrangement of words and vocal stress, his distinctive voice should emerge from the mouth of whoever is reading the poem.

Now try the same experiment with a rap verse, a verse that is comparably as sophisticated in its genre as Poe's is in his, and something altogether different occurs. Give those same ten people Nas's "One Mic." Let's assume that none of them have ever heard the song. Let's also assume that they've been given nothing but the lyrics. "All I need is one life, one try, one breath, I'm one man / What I stand for speaks for itself, they don't understand." Without hearing Nas's distinctive performance—the way his voice rises from a whisper to a shout—and without even the benefit of listening to the instrumental track, chances are they will recite it in ten different ways. Some will read it flat, with almost no added inflection at all. Others might catch a hint of Nas's syncopation, or see a cluster of syllables, or emphasize a particular stress pattern. Certainly none of them would rap it like Nas does. This begs the obvious question: What does Poe's poem have that Nas's does not, or to frame it more broadly, what does a literary verse reveal about its rhythm that a rap verse does not and why?

To answer this, it's necessary to return to rap's dual rhythmic relationship. The rhythm of rap's poetry, you'll recall, is defined by that fundamental relationship between the regularity of the beat and the liberated irregularity of the rapper's flow. Literary verse, by contrast, concerns itself with rhythm and meter. It goes without saying that when composing *Annabel Lee* the only beat Poe worked with was the particular metric ideal he had in mind. It was contingent, then, upon Poe to represent on the page both his idiosyncratic rhythm and the vestiges of the ideal meter from which it came. To put it another way, Poe has to be both the rapper and his own beatbox all at once.

Nas, on the other hand, knows that we will likely only hear his rhymes in the particular context of the "One Mic" beat. That means that while, like Poe, he composes his lines with a regular meter in mind, his lyrics need not carry the burden of representing that meter—the beat of the instrumental track does that for him. On a practical level, this means that the range of Nas's rhythmic freedom is potentially broader than Poe's, which must stay closer to his chosen meter so that his reader never loses the beat. This doesn't mean that Nas and rappers like him have complete rhythmic autonomy. Quite the contrary, because rappers are conscious of how their lyrics function as both poetry and song, they will stay close to the rhythm laid down by the beat—the rapper's version of poetic meter.

So now give our ten readers Nas's lyrics again, but this time play them the beat, and you'll likely see a marked improvement in their reading's resemblance to Nas's performance and an increase in their similarity to one another. Given a sense of the rhythmic order against which Nas composed and performed his lines, it is easier to fit the lyrics to the beat. Indeed, it may be hard to fit them anywhere besides where Nas put them. Of course, for the nonrapper it still presents quite a challenge to rap someone else's lyrics to a beat. As an oral idiom, rap's rhythm only partly exists on the page; it requires the beat and the distinctive rhythmic sensibility of the lyricist to make it whole.

A lyrical transcription rarely provides all the information needed to reconstruct a rapper's flow. Without the benefit of the beat, we are left to guess at how the words fit together and upon what syllables the stresses fall. If we try to read a rhyme in the same way we would a literary verse—that is, with our minds attuned to the metrical clues imbedded in the lines themselves—we are likely only to approximate the MC's actual performance; rappers, far more frequently than literary poets, accentuate unusual syllables in their verses. Consider the following example from the opening lines of Jay-Z's 1998 hit "Can I Get A. . . ." Keep in mind that Jay-Z is generally considered to have a conversational flow, one that falls comfortably into conventional speech rhythms.

However, when presented with a beat that challenges his natural cadence, Jay-Z responds by crafting a flow that emulates the track's pulsating tempo.

> Can I hit it in the morning
> without giving you half of my dough
> and even worse if I was broke would you want me?

Without having heard the beat or Jay-Z's idiosyncratic flow, one would be hopelessly lost in discerning the precise pattern of accented syllables. One likely could not, for instance, discern the following unusual stresses that Jay-Z gives to his performance:

> Can I hit it in the **MOR**ning
> without giving you half of my dough
> and even worse if I was broke would you **WANT** me?

By exaggerating the penultimate syllables in the first and third lines, he not only achieves a distinctive rhythm but actually creates the illusion of a *rhyme* where no rhyme exists ("morning" and "want me"). This is only possible in oral expression; it depends upon the interrelatedness of two spoken words and the relation of that same pair of words to the beat. For a rapper whose style is normally distinguished by its conversational quality, such self-conscious artifice is a testament to his rhythmic versatility—or, as Jigga himself might say, to his ability to switch up his flow.

It is worth emphasizing again that both a rapper's ability to fashion a rhythm pattern *and* to depart from that pattern are equally important to a rapper's flow. Both of these factors are ultimately conditioned by the beat's tempo and the variety of musical elements on the track. This is the reason that rap songs are almost always produced with a rapper writing rhymes to a beat rather than with a producer making a beat to a rapper's lyrics. The rhythm of the human voice is adaptable in ways the beat is not; a slight slip-up in the voice is usually of little consequence, while in the beat the results can be disastrous.

When a rapper's flow is fully realized, it forges a distinctive rhythmic identity that is governed both by poetic and musical laws. There is a tendency to associate flow almost exclusively with the smooth, liquid rhythms of MCs like Big Daddy Kane or LL Cool J. Flow includes the idea of effortlessness, of not struggling against the beat but working within it to accentuate the rhythm in human tones. Sometimes MCs' flows can so dominate their styles that they overshadow other elements of craft. For instance, Black Thought, the prodigious lyricist for the Roots, has a powerfully rhythmic flow that marks his signature rhyme style. Set within the complex soundscapes offered up by the rest of the group, Black Thought's liquid flow at times nearly washes away his meaning.

Could it be, then, that a rapper's flow could be too smooth? Could flow potentially compromise poetic complexity in rhyme, wordplay, or other elements of style? In an insightful interview with *The Guardian*, British rapper the Streets makes a reasonable case for the potential excesses of flow. "What you find with a lot of rappers is they work out their flow—the rhythm to their words—and the better they get, the more tidy the flow becomes, until everything has to fit in, the same way it would with a poem," he argues. "But I tend to think that if it all gets too tidy, the words don't really stick in your mind when you hear them—the smoothness of the rhythm makes you lose concentration." Listen to the Streets for any amount of time and it is clear that he practices what he preaches. What stands out about his flow is the way it *refuses* to flow. Like water through leaky pipes, his lyrics alternately spill out and clog up in relation to the beat. At times he defiantly sets his flow against the rhythmic direction of the rest of the song. Just when you wonder whether he's even heard the beat at all, he finds his way back in the pocket for a moment, only to jump out again.

What all of these examples tell us is that rap's poetry articulates itself in music. Flow takes its meaning from its musical context. While lyrical transcription can reveal a great deal about rap's poetic form and rhythms, it is but an intermediary step that must ultimately lead us back to the performance itself. Nowhere is this more obvious than with MCs that rely upon their delivery above all else to define their style. One such artist is Twista.

In 1991 a rapper from the west side of Chicago named Tung Twista released his debut album on Loud Records, *Runnin' Off at da Mouth*. While it was only a modest hit, it earned him mention in the *Guinness Book of World Records* as the world's fastest rapper. He would lose the title, regain it, and then lose it again, but it was clear that he was one of a rare breed of speed rappers. The fraternity of speed rappers includes artists as different from one another as Bone Thugs-N-Harmony, Big Daddy Kane, and OutKast, all of whom occasionally rapped at tempos that stretched the bounds of human breath control. Few, however, were as committed to speed rapping as Tung Twista. Eventually he would lose the

"Tung," and with it, his monomaniacal focus on speed rapping. Twista's platinum-selling 2004 album *Kamikaze* displayed an expanded array of lyrical skills, not to mention a variety of tempos for his flow.

Whether rhyming slowly or quickly, though, tempo is a defining element of rap rhythm, responsible for shaping the distinctive cadences of an MC's signature flow. Tempo is sound over time. Reflecting on his past as a speed rapper, Twista recognizes that certain necessary constraints must govern a rapper's tempo. "I think a lot of artists that rap or want to rap in that style focus more on the speed and the style than they do the clarity," he explained to *MTV News* in 2005. "They've got it locked in their mind 'I want to do it fast' or 'I want to do it like this,' but with me I always go about the clarity first, and if I couldn't say it [clearly] I'm not gonna write it. . . . If I can't get it all the way out or make it sound crisp or it's not within my vocal range or something, I won't even mess with it." An MC's cadence, then, is governed in part by the possibilities presented by sound over time. Flow is defined by rap's respect for clarity, and even the limitations of the rapper's instrument: the human voice.

When given a beat upon which to rhyme, the beats per minute present the rapper with the minimum, optimal, and maximum syllable load. As an oral idiom, rap is governed by these physical constraints of the human voice. Breath control shapes rhythmic possibilities just as much as an MC's lyrical imagination. Like singers, rappers must understand and practice effective vocal phrasing. Phrasing is all the more significant given that, more than most other forms of popular music, rap emphasizes clarity. Rappers have ways, of course, of making the language malleable and easing the challenges of breath control. The most common of these is altered pronunciation. Sometimes an MC will say just enough of a word to make it clearly discernable before going right into the next phrase, all the while staying on beat. Other times they will employ dramatic pauses, for both artistic emphasis and practical necessity. All of these subtle but essential changes take place on rap's microscopic level: the syllable.

The English language contains thirty-five sounds and twenty-six letters. Somehow, out of all of this, rhymes are born. "If, in rap, rhythm is more significant than harmony or melody, it is rhythm dependent on language, on the ways words rhyme and syllables count," writes Simon Frith. A syllable is the basic organizational unit for a sequence of speech sounds; it is the phonological building block of language. Sometimes a single syllable can form a word—like "cat" or "bat." More often, it is combined with other syllables to form multisyllabic words. Syllables matter to rap for several reasons. They partly dictate rap's rhythms based upon the natural syllabic emphasis of spoken language. In literary verse, syllabic prosody relies upon the number of syllables in the poetic line without regard to stress. Haiku, for instance, follows this method. Most modern poetry in English, however, favors accentual meter—poetry that patterns itself on stressed syllables alone. Stress, as we discussed earlier, is the vocal emphasis accorded each syllable relative to the emphasis given to those around it. The English language naturally contains so many stresses that no other organizational principle for meter makes sense.

Manipulating the numbers of syllables can function quite effectively in rap. Rakim, one of rap's greatest rhyme innovators, emphasizes the importance of an MC's control of language on the smallest possible levels. "My style of writing, I love putting a lot of words in the bars, and it's just something I started doing," he explains. "Now it's stuck with me. I like being read. The way you do that is by having a lot of words, a lot of syllables, different types of words." Charting the number of syllables in the lines of a given rap verse is a useful technique. By doing so, one notices patterns of repetition and difference. In the lines that follow, Eminem creates a syllabic pattern of around ten syllables, which he then disrupts by expanding the number of syllables to nearly double by the end. "Drug Ballad," from which these lines are drawn, is a study in breath control and lyrical artistry at the microscopic level of syllable.

> Back when Mark Wahlberg was Marky Mark, (9 syllables)
> this is how we used to make the party start. (11)
> We used to . . . mix in with Bacardi Dark (10)
> and when it . . . kicks in you can hardly talk (10)
> and by the . . . sixth gin you gon' probably crawl (10)
> and you'll be . . . sick then and you'll probably barf (10)
> and my pre . . . diction is you gon' probably fall (11)
> either somewhere in the lobby or the hallway wall (13)
> and every . . . thing's spinnin' you're beginning to think
>   women (14)
> are swimmin' in pink linen again in the sink (12)
> then in a couple of minutes that bottle of Guinness is
>   finished . . . (17)

To perform this last line without breaking his flow, Eminem increases the tempo of his delivery and alters his prosody (his pitch, length, timbre, etc.). The contrast between syllabic order and syllabic overflow creates an effective and pleasing structural pattern that listeners experience primarily on the level of rhythm. After listening to this track, try tapping out the natural beat of the syllables. The rhythm you'll hear is the skeleton of Eminem's flow. The difference between that tapping and what you hear when Eminem rhymes is best defined in the last elements of flow that we shall discuss, pattern and performance.

One usually does not think of nineteenth-century Jesuit poet-priests and hip hop at the same time, but English poet Gerard Manley Hopkins has something to teach us about flow. In a famous line from his journals, he describes his discovery of "sprung rhythm." In technical terms, sprung rhythm is a variant of strong-stress meter in which each metric foot begins with a stressed syllable, which can stand alone or relate to anywhere from one to three—and even more— unstressed syllables. Hopkins demarcated this stressed syllable with an accent mark to instruct his readers to give the syllable extra emphasis. For instance, in *The Wreck of the Deutschland*, he wrote the following line: "The sour scythe cringe, and the blear share cóme." When the line is read naturally, "come" does not get emphasis, but by imposing emphasis on it, Hopkins established an unexpected and powerful rhythm pattern in his verse.

For rap's purposes, what matters is not only Hopkins's formal innovation, but his particular account of how it came about. In a journal entry dated July 24, 1866, he recorded the following: "I had long had haunting my ear the echo of a new rhythm which now I realised on paper. . . . I do not say the idea is altogether new . . . but no one has professedly used it and made it the principle throughout, that I know of. . . . However, I had to mark the stresses . . . and a great many

more oddnesses could not but dismay an editor's eye, so that
when I offered it to our magazine *The Month* . . . they dared
not print it." That rhythm can haunt us with its power is un-
deniable. If you doubt it, simply listen to some Brazilian
samba or to Max Roach's cadence on "Valse Hot." That
rhythm can haunt us in words, however, is something else
entirely, something that requires the poet's attention.

As it was for Hopkins, rhythm is often born for MCs long
before the right words arrive. "Once I figure out in my mind
that it's going to go 'da da da dadada da da,'" Bun B says,
"then it's kind of like filling in the blanks. . . . I take the typ-
ical words, or I pick a two-word, three-word pattern." Like
Hopkins, MCs face the challenge of communicating a felt
rhythm in the medium of language. In *The Art of Emceeing*, a
self-published handbook for aspiring MCs, Stic.man from the
group dead prez writes that rappers often begin composing a
rhyme by scatting, much like jazz singers—using sequences of
nonsense syllables to improvise vocal rhythms over the music. This frees an MC to try out different flows for a given
beat before actually writing a rhyme. Such a technique sim-
plifies the experience of rapping by stripping it down to its
most basic element: rhythm. Having generated a range of
flows that work well with the beat, an MC might then go
about developing the other figurative, thematic, and narrative elements of a verse. Inspiration for flows is all around
the rapper who would keep an open mind and open ears.
Stic.man even advises aspiring MCs to study the patterns of
high-hat drums in Latin, jazz, and African music to find new
ways of relating their voices to the beat.

Of course the haunting rhythm that compels an MC to
rhyme is as individual as the given artist. In the hip-hop industry beats by a producer—9th Wonder, for instance—

might circulate to numerous rappers before they find a home. Many factors go into the selection process (market forces and trends in popularity being foremost), but one would hope that the MC's inspiration to rhyme to that particular beat would factor somewhere into the equation. Other times, the beat chooses the MC—or, more specifically, a producer tailors a beat to fit the distinctive vocal qualities and style of a given rapper. In an invaluable glimpse into the craft of producing, the RZA describes his own beat-making principles:

> In early hip-hop a lot of the beats were made by a producer with his idea of what a beat is, not an MC's idea. So musically it might sound good, but it doesn't inspire that feeling in an MC, that spark that makes him want to grab a mike and rip it. I felt that, when you're producing hip-hop, you want the vocals to *be* the instrument. Get out of the way.

A beat at its best is a reason to rhyme. It is the "spark that makes him [or her] want to grab a mike and rip it" by insinuating a personal sense of rhythm onto the track by means of a distinctive flow. The best way of illustrating this individuated relationship between an MC and a beat is to listen to different artists rhyming on the same track.

An excellent, if underappreciated, demonstration of the rhythmic versatility that two rappers can achieve on a single beat is Ludacris's guest-performance on Cee-Lo's song "Childz Play" from his 2000 release, *Cee-Lo Green . . . Is the Soul Machine*. Cee-Lo is a former member of the Atlanta rap collective Goodie Mob and, most recently, the vocal half of Gnarls Barkley, the group responsible for the 2006 worldwide hit "Crazy." He is also a skilled lyricist with a striking rhythmic sensibility. "Childz Play" finds both Cee-Lo and Ludacris in excellent form. The instrumental track sounds like a kind of funkafied cartoon theme song, complete with intricate xylophone and harpsichord loops. The beat, in an unusual 3/4 time signature, is a deliberately paced back-and-forth bounce with a walking bass line and a snapping snare drum, but the overall effect of the track is frenetic thanks to the blazing notes of its samples. Cee-Lo rhymes first using a highly stylized, stop-start flow that bobs and weaves as he verbally jabs the track. Even without the music, one can see in the transcription his distinctive patterning of two and three syllable phrases:

> Well, hello. Howdy do? How are you? That's good.
> Who me? I'm still hot, I still got, you got me?
> I'm here, I'm there, 'cause I'm raw, 'cause I'm rare.
> I can spit on anything, got plenty game, authentic.
> My pen's sick, forensic, defends it, he wins it
> Again and a, again and a, again and a, again and a

In the above lines and throughout the verse, Cee-Lo revises the pattern he establishes by both emphasizing the discrete rhythmic units through repetition and distinguishing them by juxtaposing phrases and single words that share the same number of syllables in polysyllabic rhymes—"authentic" and "my pen's sick," for example. While most of the rhythm units are two and three syllables long, he includes a pair of four syllable phrases ("on anything" and "got plenty game") and then concludes with a four-syllable phrase repeated four times. The overall effect of his flow is to emphasize the speed of the track, making the beat seem as if it is faster than it actually is.

Compare Cee-Lo's flow with Ludacris's opening lines from the next verse, keeping in mind that the tempo of the beat remains exactly the same:

> . . . Who the only little nigga
> that you know with bout fifty flows, do about fifty shows
> in a week but creep on the track with my tippy toes
> Shhh! Shut the fuck up, I'm trying to work.
> Ah forget it, I'm going berserk.
> 'Cause I stack my change, and I'm back to claim
> my reign on top, so pack your things.
> I've racked your brain like crack cocaine.
> My fame won't stop or I'll jack your chain.

In contrast to Cee-Lo's opening, Ludacris begins halfway through a measure, spilling directly into the next (as rendered above by the ellipses and the enjambment of the first and second lines). Where Cee-Lo chops up ordinary speech patterns in unusual syllabic units, Ludacris runs his syllables together by emphasizing—and accelerating—normal speech patterns. The producer underscores Ludacris's distinct rhythmic approach by dropping out the musical loops to leave only voice, drums, and bass line. The combined effect is that the tempo, which Cee-Lo's stop-start flow had rendered so fast, now seems to have slowed to a saunter. What has changed is not the tempo of the beat, however, only the rhythm of the rapper's flow. By the fifth line, Ludacris begins employing stronger accents ("I'm going ber-zerk"). His flow even begins to resemble Cee-Lo's cadence. The rhythm is now ordered not by natural speech stresses but by creative pairings of syllables. Look at these lines again with the stressed syllables marked:

'Cause I **STACK** my change, and I'm **BACK** to claim
my reign on top, so **PACK** your things.
I've **WRACKED** your brain like **CRACK** cocaine.
My fame won't stop or I'll **JACK** your chain.

Ludacris patterns this section of his verse on an economy
of stressed syllables, no more than three and usually two per
line. In addition to the naturally accented syllables ("reign"
and "top," for instance), Ludacris uses overaccented syllables—
all rhyming the same sound ("ack"). All of these fall in relation to the beat so as to create a rhythmic balance alongside
the snare's accentuation of the one and three. What results is
a playful flow that emphasizes the back-and-forth momen-
tum of the track even as it creates its own rhythmic logic
through its patterns of emphasis. Within a span of only a
handful of lines, Ludacris shows us at least two of his "fifty
flows," and demonstrates the possibilities each beat opens up
for an imaginative MC.

Whenever they perform rappers make a series of complex
poetic decisions—not the least of which involves rhythm.
"Crafting a good flow is like doing a puzzle," Stic.man explains. "In a rap lyric the syllables, pauses, pronunciation,
wit, energy of our performance and tempo, all determine the
parameters of what is a 'good' flow or not." Both Cee-Lo and
Ludacris demonstrate "good" flows, as different as they may
be from one another. The point is, while a beat may set the
boundaries of a rap's rhythm, rappers still have tremendous
freedom to find a place for themselves in the groove. Once
there, they are far from finished; they must then attend to
the linguistic purpose of hip-hop poetry: the rhyme itself.

TWO **Rhyme**

RHYME IS THE music MCs make with their mouths. When T. J. Swan sings the title line on Biz Markie's "Make the Music with Your Mouth, Biz," he's not just telling Biz to beatbox, he's inviting him to rock the mic with rhymes. While some MCs are also known for singing with melody and harmony—Mos Def and Lauryn Hill come to mind— most rappers don't sing at all. What they do instead is rhyme in a cadence. Rhyming words gives rap its song, underscoring the small but startling music of language itself.

Everyone knows rhyme when they hear it, but few stop to examine it. Rhyme is the concordance of sound. It works by establishing a habit of expectation in listeners' minds, conditioning them to identify patterns of sound, to connect words the mind instinctively recognizes as related yet distinct.

All rhyme relies on the innate human impulse to recognize patterns and to anticipate what will follow. A skillfully rendered rhyme strikes a balance between expectation and novelty.

It might be useful to think of rap rhyme on a sliding scale of listener expectation, with one end representing unwavering rhyme regularity and the other no rhyme at all. Either extreme leads to collapse, but between them is a wide range of possibilities that satisfy the listener's desire for rhyme. Free-verse rap, rap that does not rhyme at all, is rare, if not nonexistent. At the same time, rap that rhymes incessantly and perfectly soon grows tiresome.

The most common rap rhymes are end rhymes, those rhymes that fall on the last beat of the musical measure, signaling the end of the poetic line. Two lines in succession with end rhymes comprise a couplet, the most common rhyme scheme in old-school rap. In addition to defining the line, rhyme serves a secondary purpose of organizing rhythm by dividing sound into recognizable units. "Along with word choice and sound patterns, the sound effects of rhyme and repetition help create the rhythm of a poem," notes Frances Mayes. "Recurrence of a sound is itself a music. Like the chorus in a song, a refrain or rhyming pattern, once set up, rewards our anticipation."

Rhyme is the reason we can begin to hear a rhythm just by reading these lines from 50 Cent's 2007 hit "I Get Money": "Get a tan? I'm already black. Rich? I'm already that / Gangsta, get a gat, hit a head in a hat / Call that a riddle rap. . . ." The first line establishes a pattern of stressed syllables in successive phrases ("al*rea*dy **black**, al*rea*dy **that**") that he carries over into the next two lines ("**get** a **gat**, **hit** a *head, in* a *hat, ri*ddle *rap*"). Three of these four phrases end in rhymes, one a perfect rhyme ("gat" and "hat") and the third a slant rhyme ("rap"). The overall effect of the performance rewards our anticipation by balancing expectation and surprise in its sounds.

Rhyming renders familiar words unexpected and fresh. Whether falling at the end of lines or cropping up somewhere in the middle, rhymes result in heightened, artificial, almost ceremonial remixes of everyday speech. Rap's rhymes rely heavily on the oral tradition, inscribing patterns that may appear quixotic on the page but build unmistakable sonic structures when performed. For instance, chain rhymes—extended runs of the same rhyme sound over a series of lines, often with both end and internal rhymes—have become increasingly popular among MCs in recent years. As rap has evolved, the range of rhyme patterns has expanded to include a host of strategies that fulfill the listener's expectation for rhyme even as they explore new expressive possibilities. Without melody, with rhythm alone, rap organizes words into forms that are strange yet familiar to the ear.

Rap's reliance on rhyme distinguishes it from almost every other form of contemporary music and from most contemporary literary poetry. Many other genres of popular lyric can take rhyme or leave it. And in recent years, literary poetry has seemingly neglected rhyme or, if not neglected it, subsumed it more fully into its form, eschewing discernable patterns of end rhymes for subtler arrangements of internal ones.

Rap celebrates rhyme like nothing else, hearkening back to a time when literary poetry still unabashedly embraced the simple pleasure and musicality of verse. Rap rhymes so much and with such variety that it is now the largest and richest contemporary archive of rhymed words. It has done more than any other art form in recent history to expand rhyme's formal range and expressive possibilities.

Rhyme consists of the repetition of the last stressed vowel sound and all the sounds following that vowel—such as in the words "demonstrate" and "exonerate." Rhyme is the echo of sound from one word to another, an echo that simultaneously announces similarity and difference. To put it another way, rhyming words begin different but end the same. This balance between the familiar and the unfamiliar is the very spirit of rhyme. As Alfred Corn explains, "Where there is no similarity, there is no rhyme. Where the similarity is too great, boredom sets in. Skillful rhyming involves finding a balance between identity and difference."

In its most basic sense, rhyme is a sonic balance between identity (or replication) and difference that relies upon the ear's capacity to draw connections between two distinct but related sounds. When identity is absolute, MCs are "rhyming" the same word—a practice that is generally frowned upon in rap circles, but has nonetheless been employed to good effect by certain artists. On the other hand, when the difference between words is too great, no rhyme registers at all. Broadly understood, rhyme also includes a host of other linguistic strategies that rely upon the echo of sound across words. Alliteration, once called head rhyme, is older even than rhyme itself. It consists of the repetition of initial consonants, as in "Peter Piper picked a peck of pickled peppers." Similarly, assonance is the rhyming of vowel sounds alone ("How now, brown cow?"), and consonance is the duplication of consonant sounds within words, rather than necessarily at the beginning of them.

The simplest rhymes are monosyllabic, like "cat" and "bat." Disyllabic rhymes achieve a different effect, like "jelly" and "belly." Multisyllabic rhymes may be found between two words, like "vacation" and "relation"; between two equal phrases, like "stayed with us" and "played with us"; or in some combination of phrases (called a broken rhyme), like "basketball" and "took a fall." Poets may rhyme different parts of speech or the same, words with close semantic relations and those at a remove from one another. Rhymes can be perfect, or they can be imperfect (also called slant or near), like "port" and "chart" or "justice" and "hostess." Rhymes can also fall at different points and in different relations to one another along the line, from end rhymes to internal rhymes to a host of specific rhyme patterns.

Most of us were first exposed to rhyme as children through nursery rhymes or childhood songs that emphasize patterns of sound. Rhyme appeals to adults for many of the same reasons it appeals to kids, most notably because it is a source of pleasure tied to a purpose. We don't even need to be consciously aware of rhyme's purpose for it to work on us, but stopping to contemplate rhyme's reason brings many rewards.

Rhyme is no mere adornment in rap. It isn't simply a mnemonic device or a singsongy trifle. It is rap's most obvious way of remaking language, of refashioning not simply sound, but meaning as well. Rhyme works on the brain as well as the ear. A new rhyme forges a mental pathway between distinct but sonically related words and carries with it both linguistic and cognitive meaning. It invites the listener to tease out the semantic threads embedded within the sonic fabric of the words. What emerges is a simple but seismic truth: MCs don't just rhyme sounds, they rhyme ideas.

In a classic verse from 1989's "Fight the Power," Public Enemy's Chuck D spits something like a working definition of rhyme's reason: "As the rhythm's designed to bounce / What counts is that the rhyme's / Designed to fill your mind." He is, of course, speaking of "rhyme" here both as the practice of patterning sounds and as another name for the verse as a whole. In both meanings, rap's rhymes have filled our minds with many things, not all of them useful. But it is more than a matter of content—be it women and cars or prisons with bars—it is also a question of poetic form. Rhyme exercises its sound in the construction of meaning. Saying something in rhyme doesn't simply sound different from saying the same thing without rhyme, it fundamentally transforms the meaning of the expression. As the critic Alfred Corn explains, "The coincidence of sound in a pair of rhymes is a recommendation to the reader to consider the rhyming words in tandem, to see what meaning emerges from their juxtaposition. The meaning will emerge as one of affinity and opposition." Within this tension between similarity and difference, rap's expressive potential is born.

Rhyme accounts for a large part of what makes great rap great. We value rap largely according to its ingenuity: the MC's skill in saying something unexpected within a given set of formal limitations. "MCing, to me," Common once said by way of describing Eminem's lyrical excellence, "is when you hear a dude say something and you tell your homie, 'You heard what he said?'" Such virtuosity is as much about constraint as it is about creativity. Creativity without constraint is unmoored, a wandering thing that never quite settles into shape. As the poet Steve Kowit observes, "The search for a rhyme-word forces the mind out of its familiar track and onto more adventurous and unfamiliar paths. . . . End-rhyme, then, is not only a delight to the ear of the reader when used well, but a spur to the imagination of the writer."

For MCs, rhyme, along with the beat, provides the necessary formal constraints on their potentially unfettered poetic freedom. If you can say anything in any way you choose, chances are you might not say anything at all, or at least anything worth remembering. It's possible, in other words, for an artist to be too free. "The imagination wants its limits and delights in its limits," Nobel laureate Derek Walcott explains. "It finds its freedom in the definition of those limits." What can you do in the space between the line's opening and its ending in rhymed relation to the line before it, or after it, or both? How do you say what you want to say but in a way that maintains that necessary association of sound that your listeners expect? Exceptional MCs, like skilled literary poets, balance sound with sense in their rhymes.

Run-of-the-mill rappers often find themselves overwhelmed by rhyme's dual challenges of sound and sense. Instead, they relinquish control of their rhymes to one or the other. The results can be disastrous. A rapper insistent on expressing a particular meaning in particular terms may find it almost impossible to rhyme at all. Much more common, however, are those rappers so insistent on how their rhymes sound that they lose control over what they are actually saying. They spend so much time making sure that one line rhymes with the next that they fail to develop metaphors or tell stories or make observations. Often they'll resort to rhymes so soiled with use that they almost cease to register as rhymes at all, so bereft are they of that essential quality of surprise. The result is not simply rhymes that sound the same, but rhymes that say the same things.

Some rap critics, and a fair number of rap fans, have bemoaned the limited thematic range in mainstream rap in recent years. The culprit they most commonly blame is big business—the record labels, radio conglomerates, and other commercial forces that treat rap as product rather than poetry. Undoubtedly, rap's growing commodification plays a significant role in limiting the variety of lyrics we hear, and yet another answer lies in rap's rhymes themselves. When MCs settle into familiar pairs of rhyme words, they also tend to settle into familiar themes and attitudes. Someone who sets out to sound like 50 Cent will likely use many of the same rhyme words that 50 employs and, as a consequence, end up rapping about the same topics.

It's easy to spot rap's true lyrical innovators because not only will they likely be rapping about different things from everyone else, they'll be using different words to do it. Eminem, for instance, had to conceive a bunch of new rhyming words to describe the experiences of a working-class white kid from a trailer park in Detroit who rises to superstardom. Who else would think to rhyme "public housing systems" with "victim of Munchausen syndrome"? Similarly, as Andre 3000 has grown throughout his career—from southern playa to ATLien to whatever his present incarnation happens to be—the words he rhymes have grown along with him. He's gone from "pimpin' hos and slammin' Cadillac do's" to rhyming "Whole Foods" with "those fools." And who could imagine that an MC would ever associate a Hebrew language with origins in tenth-century Germany, a green leafy vegetable, and an imaginary sport from a children's book, as Asher Roth does when he rhymes "Yiddish," "spinach," and "Quidditch" on his 2008 mix tape *The Greenhouse Effect?* The point is that rhyme is not simply about the relationship of two or more words, two or more sounds—it is also about rhythm and image, storytelling, and, above all, meaning. With new rhymes come possibilities for new expressions, new ideas, and new styles that point the direction toward the future of rap's poetry.

In the hands of unskilled poets and MCs alike, rhyme can be an impediment, an awkward thing that leads to unnatural sounds and unintended meanings. But rhyme well used makes for powerful expression; it at once taps into the most primal pleasure centers of the human brain, those of sound patterning, and maintains an elevated, ceremonial distance from regular speech.

Rap rhymes are often characterized as simplistic, but nothing could be further from the truth. Over the years, rap has undergone profound shifts in the range and variety of rhymes that MCs create. Rhyme comes in numerous varieties, each with a distinct function in sound and sense. *Perfect rhyme*, also known as full rhyme or true rhyme, is rhyme where words contain the same vowel sounds (usually accented) followed by identical consonant sounds (as in "all" and "ball"). *Slant rhyme* (or imperfect rhyme) is rhyme that usually involves shared final-consonant sounds, but different vowel sounds (as in "all" and "bowl"). Rap uses both. Kurupt offered author James G. Spady this fascinating insider's look into the craft of rhyming, worth quoting at length:

Perfection of the rhymes. Like Perfection. Selection.
Interjection. Election. Dedication. Creation. Domination.
Devastation. World domination. Totally, with no Hesitation,
you know what I mean? These are perfect rhymes. . . . Really.
Silly. Philly, you know.

These are perfected rhymes. Where you could take a word
[sic] like *we will* and you connect that with a full word like *rebuild*,
you know what I mean? You got two words in *we will*. One word in
rebuild. But perfect rhyme connection is the key to writing when
you write your rhyme. And meaning too.

When you're saying something that makes sense. Them are
the keys to writing a rhyme. Perfect rhyme connection. And
style.

While perfect rhymes satisfy our rhyming mind, slant
rhymes tease us a little, denying us the satisfaction of com-
pletion. The result is often a creative tension. Literary verse
from the nineteenth century until today has witnessed the
rise of slant rhyme from an occasional variation of form to a
form in itself. Emily Dickinson is the poet most often associated with slant rhyme, but she is not alone. Poets like Gerard Manley Hopkins, W. B. Yeats, Dylan Thomas, and
Wilfred Owen have made slant rhyme an accepted part of
modern poetic practice. This speaks to the growing influence of conversational style in literary poetry, something it
shares with rap.

Slant rhymes are common in rap, just as they are in other
poetic forms found in the oral tradition. "Some artists use
line after line of slant rhyme, but because of their flow and
the way they pronounce the words, you don't even hear the
words as being slant rhymes," observe Emcee Escher and

Alex Rappaport, the authors of *The Rapper's Handbook*. Slant rhymes are in obvious display in these lines from the prodigious Michigan MC One Be Lo:

> I rock their minds like the sling shot of David do
> Liver than pay-per-view
> You couch potatoes don't believe me? Call the cable crew
> Every time I bus' kids think they on their way to school
> This grown man ain't got no time to play with you
> Theresa didn't raise a fool . . .

One Be Lo augments the perfect rhymes in his lines ("do," "crew," "you," and "school," "fool") with slant rhymes ("view" and "fool"), and all are equally satisfying. Oral expression is generally more forgiving of sonic difference, offering a wider definition of what constitutes rhyme. Rap celebrates both perfect and imperfect rhymes, often using them together to achieve subtle effects of sound and sense.

Some purists, however, are dismissive of rap's practice of employing partial or slant rhymes. Slant rhymes, they suggest, testify to a lack of discipline and originality on the part of the artist. Such criticisms, however, ignore the fact that oral poetry has always been more liberal than written verse when it comes to what constitutes rhyme. Rap, like oral poetry through the ages, goes by the ear rather than by the book.

Rap rhyme took a formal leap with the popularizing of *multisyllabic rhymes*. While rap's pioneers occasionally included a multi in their arsenal, no MC has made it a signature element of style quite like Big Daddy Kane. For Kane, the multisyllabic rhyme is a versatile tool, a way of doing things with words. He often employs it to connect a single multisyllabic word with a balanced multisyllabic phrase. He then strings together lines, sometimes in couplets, sometimes in fierce runs of the same rhyme. Compared to conventional monosyllabic rhymes, multis not only provide a broader range of possible complimentary words, but also achieve a sonic effect of speed and virtuosity.

Multis are also sometimes associated with more-complex and thus potentially less-commercial lyricism. The fear is that if the rhyme calls too much attention to itself, it will leave too little attention to the beat, or the hook, or the other elements of a song that tend to ensure mass appeal. This seems to be precisely what Lupe Fiasco is addressing on "Dumb It Down" from his 2007 album, *The Cool*. While the hook sardonically warns "You goin' over niggas' heads Lu (Dumb it down) / They tellin' me that they don't feel you (Dumb it down) / We ain't graduate from school, nigga (Dumb it down) / Them big words ain't cool, nigga (Dumb it down)," Lupe's verse defiantly demonstrates the very lyrical complexity the hook warns against:

> I'm **FEARLESS**, now **HEAR THIS**, I'm **EARLESS** (less)
> and I'm **PEERLESS** (less), which means I'm **EYELESS**
> which means I'm **TEARLESS**, which means **MY IRIS**
> resides where my **EARS IS**, which means I'm blinded

Lupe relies on multis to render the kind of abstract rhymes that flout the warnings of the hook. In four lines he delivers eight multis—some perfect, some slant; some individual words, some two-word phrases.

For range and quality of multisyllabic rhymes, one contemporary artist comes to mind: Pharoahe Monch. On the standout track "Simon Says" from his solo debut, Pharoahe spits this series of multis:

> You all up in the Range and shit **INEBRIATED**
> Phased from your original plan, you **DEVIATED**
> I **ALLEVIATED** the pain, with a long-term **GOAL**
> Took my underground loot, without the **GOLD**

He begins by rhyming three words likely never before rhymed in the history of rap, "inebriated," "deviated," and "alleviated," then caps it off with a slant rhyme, "goal" and "gold," for good measure. He does all of this without sacrificing meaning or getting forced into unintended expressions.

Some of the most formally sophisticated rhymes often escape notice, in large part because they work so well. After all, the reason MCs conceive elaborate rhymes in the first place is not to show how clever they are, but to put words together in such a way that they do something to the listener. One of the most reliable ways, therefore, to uncover poetically innovative lyrics is to pay close attention to those lines that stick in your head, that just *sound* right. Like any rap fan, I have many such lines stored in my mental catalog. They'll come to me at all times during the day—while I'm at the gym or out to dinner, sometimes even while I'm lecturing in class. As students of rap's poetry, we do well to listen to this intuitive part of our critical intelligence; it is often a truer guide than our more intellectualized thought process. That intuitive sense brought me to these lines from Pharoahe Monch, part of another virtuosic verse from his first album:

The *LAST* **BATTER** to *HIT*, *BLAST*, **SHATTER**ed your *HIP*
Smash any *SPLIT*ter or *FAST*ball, that'll be *IT*

Condensed within these sonically packed two lines, Pharoahe Monch constructs a rich texture of sound variations. The verse as a whole is dominated by this same energy of insistent repetition—from perfect rhymes to assonance and consonance—delivering on the promise he makes in the song's hook of presenting "the next millennium rap." In the above lines, he employs a rhyme variation called *apocopated rhyme*, where a one-syllable word rhymes with the stressed portion of a multisyllabic word (like "dance" and "*romanc*ing"). In this case, he matches the first line's monosyllabic internal rhymes, "last" and "blast," with an apocopated rhyme, "*fast*ball," on the next line. He does the same thing in reverse with another rhyme sound as well, using "hit" to form an apocopated rhyme with "*split*ter" and a perfect rhyme with "it." This creates a formal structure of rhyme that binds the two lines together. Add to that the slant rhyme of "hip," the assonance on the long *a* sound ("last," "batter," "blast," "shattered," "smash," "fast," "that") and the consonance on the *t* sound, and you have a couplet where almost every word is doing some kind of rhyme work.

Not surprisingly, the rhymes in these lines also shape the rhythm, with a pattern of stress carrying over from phrase to phrase ("batter to hit" with "shattered your hip" and "that'll be it"). Notice how the lines retain structure even when the words themselves are removed:

Duh Da **DA-DA DUH DA**, Da **DA-DA DUH DA**
Da Duh-duh da da duh da-da, **DA-DA DUH DA**

In these lines rhyme not only functions as adornment, but as a guide for Pharoahe's flow. Such syllabic patterning, using rhyme to fashion a rhythm, has become increasingly common in rap over the years, with artists as different from one another as Cam'ron and Eminem taking full advantage of its effects.

Pharoahe Monch's verse is the work of a poetic technician, to be sure, but what makes it also the work of a virtuoso is that the lyrics are completely unburdened by the potentially ponderous weight of this intricate structure. On the page and, even more, in the performance, the lines gain an effortless, almost offhanded eloquence that liberates the listener to enjoy the line in the sound alone. Looking behind the rhymes takes none of that pleasure away. What it does instead is add a measure of respect to the craft of fitting rhymes to beats.

MC's inevitably run up against the boundaries of expressive possibility through rhyming two words together. In response, they often employ rhyme techniques that cross the limits of word pairs to fashion rhyme groupings made up of several words that relate to one another in rhyme. The Notorious B.I.G. does this on "Who Shot Ya": "Saw me in the drop, three and a **quarter** / **Slaughter**, electrical tape around your **daughter**." Blending end rhyme and internal rhyme, Biggie creates an aural sensation that emphasizes the key words in the lines.

By contrast, *broken rhyme*, or split rhyme, involves rhyming a single multisyllabic word with several monosyllabic words. In the Western poetic tradition, such a technique is most often employed for comic effect, as it is in these famous lines from Canto XXII of Lord Byron's *Don Juan:*

"But—Oh! ye lords of ladies *intellectual*, / Inform us truly, have they not *hen-peck'd you all?*" As the punch line for the canto, Byron's playful rhyme underscores the humor of the lines. In contrast to the more conventional perfect rhymes in the lines that precede it ("wed," "bred," and "head"), the broken rhyme delights the ear.

But where broken rhymes were nearly always played for comic purposes in literary verse, rap has made them a commonplace element of its poetics. Rap has given broken rhymes a new and larger life. Like multis, broken rhymes have becomes more pervasive and versatile as rap poetics has developed. So while we might hear a broken rhyme like this from Melle Mel on "White Lines," "Ticket to ride a white line *highway* / Tell all your friends that they can go *my way*," we get a more inventive use of the technique when the Notorious B.I.G. boasts on "Hypnotize," "*escargot, my car go* one-sixty, swiftly." The difference is that Melle Mel's example is intuitive, even obvious, while Biggie's is unexpected and fresh. Not surprisingly Big Daddy Kane, the master of the multi, was also fond of broken rhymes. On "Wrath of Kane," he unleashes a swarm:

> 'Cause I never let 'em **ON TOP OF ME**
> I play 'em out like a game of **MONOPOLY**
> Let us beat around the ball like an **ASTRO**
> Then send 'em to jail for tryin to **PASS GO**
> Shakin' 'em up, breakin' 'em up, takin' no stuff,
> But it still ain't loud enough . . .

In both Biggie's and Kane's rhymes, the intended effect is far from comic. Certainly there's an unmistakable playfulness in Biggie's enumeration of his riches—the fancy snails contrasting with the fast and fancy cars—but the broken rhyme is less about comic relief than it is about evincing a self-aware rhyme virtuosity. The same holds for Kane. In a verse where he is extolling his lyrical excellence, the broken rhymes manifest that very excellence with audible evidence.

A host of effects accompany rhyme, all relying upon the echo of sound across poetic lines. *Alliteration* is the repetition of initial consonant sound. It is older even than rhyme itself. In the following lines from *Piers Plowman*, written in the fourteenth century, alliteration works to underscore the music of language itself:

> A feir feld ful of folk fold I ther bi-twene,
> Of alle maner of men, the men and the riche . . .

Repetition has reached almost to the point of parody here; indeed, in a contemporary piece of writing, it would be difficult to read these lines as anything else. Such sonic effects can come in subtler forms as well. When alliteration occurs at different places within words rather than simply at the beginning, we call it *consonance*. These lines from John Milton's *Paradise Lost* show alliteration (the h sound) and consonance (the d and the g sounds) working together to achieve a common effect:

> **H**eaven opene**d** wi**d**e
> **H**er ever-**d**uring **g**ates, **h**armonious sound
> On **g**olden **h**inges of movin**g** . . .

The sonic repetitions in Milton's lines are at once unob-trusive yet inescapable; they underscore a unity of thought and expression. Consonance such as this is quite often em-ployed in rap, whether to underscore rhyme or to offer a kind of rhyme substitute. Lauryn Hill's lines from the Fugees' "Zealots" show consonance at work alongside rhyme:

> Rap rej*ec*ts my tape d*eck*, ej*ec*ts proj*ectile*
> Whether Jew or Gent*ile*, I rank top percent*ile*
> Many st*yle*s, more powerful than **gamma rays**
> My **grammar pays** like Carlos **Santana plays**

Consonance with one sound ("eck") shifts to multisyllabic rhymes with another sound ("projectile," "Gentile," "per-centile") and then another ("gamma rays," "grammar pays," "Santana plays"). The result is as intricate as it is effortless.

A related linguistic technique is *assonance*, which relies upon the replication of unaccented vowel sounds. Its pur-pose in oral expression is to delight the ear, but also to center the listener's attention on a given set of lines. Often the ex-ercise of assonance is imperceptible, though its subconscious effect is almost always pronounced, helping to generate a subtle mood or tone. Consider the effect assonance has on these lines from John Keats's *Ode on a Grecian Urn* (1820): "Thou still unravished bride of quietness, / Thou foster child of silence and slow time." Its long *i* sound extenuates the sound of the line beyond its actual bounds, adding an unmis-takable languorous quality.

In rap, one of the masters of these techniques of sonic identity is Eminem. Eminem's style favors both assonance and alliteration; he has elevated them to an art. In the fol-lowing lines, a guest verse on "Renegade," a track Eminem produced for Jay-Z's *The Blueprint* (2001), Eminem demon-strates a virtuoso's control of sound and sense.

> Now who's the king of these rude ludicrous lucrative lyrics
> Who could inherit the title, put the youth in hysterics
> Using his music to steer it, sharing his views and his merits
> But there's a huge interference—they're saying you shouldn't
>   hear it

Rhyme, at least full rhyme, is almost absent from this verse, replaced instead by the concordance of sound. Asso-nance, the repetition of vowel sounds, is the governing struc-ture here; he packs no fewer than thirty-seven instances of it into the full verse's twenty lines (the *u* sound predominates). When he does employ rhyme, it is most often slant. Perhaps the most striking instance of this is the chain of interlocking slant rhymes, both internal and end rhymes, that spans the lines quoted above ("lyrics," "inherit," "hysterics," "steer it," "merits," "interference," "hear it"). Those who doubt the conscious artistry exercised by rap's greatest MCs need look no further than these lines for evidence of its vitality.

When rhyme and all of its allied forms are at work in a single performance, the effect is often unforgettable. In 1995, shortly after leaving prison, Tupac Shakur released what would become perhaps his best-known song, "California Love." It reached number one on the *Billboard* charts, and *Rolling Stone* included it as Tupac's sole entry in its 2004 list of the five hundred greatest songs of all time. Produced by Dr. Dre, who also spits the first verse, the song is driven by an infectious piano riff and a catchy hook performed by Roger Troutman of Zapp and Roger. All of this would likely have made it a hit; Tupac made it a classic. His opening lines are among the most unmistakable in all of rap:

> Out on **BAIL** fresh outta **JAIL**, California ***DREAMIN'***
> Soon as I stepped on the scene, I'm hearin' hoochies
> ***SCREAMIN'***

In just two lines, Tupac combines rhyme (both end and internal), assonance, and alliteration to create a feeling of tension and energy. The first line includes three rhyme elements: a monosyllabic internal rhyme ("bail" and "jail") and the first part of a multisyllabic rhyme ("dreamin'," which he rhymes in the next line with "screamin'"). Along with this, he includes alliteration with the s and h sounds. Almost every word is somehow sonically connected with some other word in the lines. Hip-hop fans often talk about an MC sounding "hungry," the necessity with which they're driven to express themselves. These may be the hungriest two lines in rap history.

Rhyme, alliteration, assonance, and consonance combined often produce tongue-twisting linguistics. Big Punisher's "Twinz" includes this couplet, as inspired in its way as Tupac's lines. "Dead in the middle of little Italy / Little did we know that we riddled a middle man who didn't know diddly." Like a jazz sax run or a scat riff, Pun's lyrical delivery balances sound with sense, using the full array of rhyme techniques to underscore the rhythm of his flow. Keying in on a single sound, he runs a staggering series of rhyme variations ("middle," "little," "riddled," "middle," "diddly"), which he further builds upon with consonance (*d*) and assonance (*i*) and alliteration (*d* and *l*). This is what happens when a poet is in complete control of his or her rhymes.

Sometimes, however, rhyme can take control, leading the poet to unintended and unwanted expressions. This is what John Milton feared when he spoke of rhyme as "a constraint to express many things otherwise, and for the most part worse, than else they would have exprest them." Not surprisingly, he includes not a single end rhyme in *Paradise Lost*. A generation before Milton, the English poet Thomas Campion warned in 1602 that the "popularitie of Rime creates as many Poets as a hot summer flies." Rhyme, he argued, could actually impede good poetry.

All rhyme, after all, is a kind of coercion: The poet forces the audience to connect disparate words and reconcile them, both in sound and meaning. Of course, as mentioned before, this accounts for a great deal of the pleasure to be had in rhyme: that process of recognition and differentiation and the balance achieved between them. But what happens when poets are overwhelmed by rhyme's coercive force—when, either for the purposes of sound or sense, poets find themselves with few rhyming options for a given word? Maybe the MC uses a word, like "pizza" or "olive," that doesn't have a perfect rhyme to fit it. Or maybe the problem is that the perfect rhyme comes too easily, and too obviously.

There was a time when Lexus was the car of choice in hip hop; it seemed like every MC was rhyming "Lexus" with "Texas"—for no other reason than it is one of the few words that rhyme with "Lexus." Whether Lexus became less popular among rappers or the rhyme became too predictable (or both), you rarely hear this pairing nowadays. But it demonstrates an important tension in rhyme: the problem of overdetermination.

Overdetermined rhymes are those that the MC or poet chooses not out of conscious design but out of desperate necessity or lackadaisical passivity. Overdetermined rhymes are in effect forced upon the poet by the limits of language itself rather than emerging out of the imaginative use of language as a tool. They signal the loss of poetic control.

For an MC and literary poet alike, it is almost always a bad thing if the audience can complete your rhyme. This suggests that your rhyme lacks freshness, which is essential to powerful communication. Artists in any genre that employs rhyme face a similar challenge. One lyricist who has given a tremendous amount of thought to the process of rhyme composition is Bob Dylan. Dylan alongside rappers may be an unlikely combination, but it is fitting. Like the best MCs, Dylan revels in the ingenuity of his rhymes. He offers a striking insight into the mind of a rhyming lyricist, in the midst of the "unconscious frame of mind" necessary for the artistic process:

> Staying in the unconscious frame of mind, you can pull yourself out and throw up two rhymes first and work it back. You get the rhymes first and work it back and then see if you can make it make sense in another kind of way. You can still stay in the unconscious frame of mind to pull it off, which is the state of mind you have to be in anyway.

For Dylan and for rap's rhyme animals, the process of lyrical composition is fundamentally a process of rhyming. "It gives you a thrill to rhyme something you might think, well, that's never been rhymed before," Dylan told an interviewer. "But then again, people have taken rhyming now, it doesn't have to be exact anymore. Nobody's going to care if you rhyme 'represent' with 'ferment,' you know. Nobody's gonna care." Dylan's remarks point the way towards rap's rhyme revolution, its expansion of rhyme's formal possibilities in the face of overdetermination and the loss of meaning.

MCs have found many ways around rhyme's restrictions. While perfect (or full) rhymes still play an important role in rap's poetics, they increasingly exist in the context of a host of other rhyme strategies. We've already looked at slant, multisyllabic, and broken rhymes, but another category is intentionally forced rhymes, what I'll term *transformative rhymes*. Transformative rhymes start with words that only partially rhyme or don't rhyme at all and alter the pronunciation to fashion perfect rhymes. For an example outside of rap, think of these famous lyrics from Arlo Guthrie's "Coming into Los Angeles," once heard at Woodstock: "Coming into Los Angeles / bringing in a couple of keys / Don't touch my bags if you please / Mister Customs Man." Guthrie fashions a transformative rhyme when he playfully alters the emphasis and pronunciation of "Los Angeleez" to forge perfect rhymes with the words that follow, "keys" and "please."

Rap often takes these transformations of pronunciation to the extreme. On "So Many Tears" Tupac delivers the following lines: "My life is in denial, and when I die / Baptized in eternal fire." They look straightforward enough on the page, but in the performance he makes "fire" rhyme with "denial" by essentially pronouncing it "file." The transformation achieves a pleasing echo of sound across the lines without sacrificing comprehension. Similarly, the Notorious B.I.G. artfully demonstrates this technique by refashioning language through rhyme on "Juicy":

> We used to fuss when the landlord **DISSED US**
> No heat, wonder why **CHRISTMAS MISSED US**.
> **BIRTHDAYS** was the **WORST DAYS**
> Now we sip champagne when we **THIRST-AY**

In the course of four lines, he offers two sets of multisyllabic rhymes; first, "dissed us," "Christmas," and "missed us," and next "birthdays," "worst days," and "thirst-ay." It is with this last rhyme that he demonstrates the creative capacity to use rhyme's restrictions in his poetic favor, adding flavor to the verse by forcing "thirsty" just this side of its breaking point to rhyme with the two words before it.

Kanye West has made such forced rhymes an important part of his poetic style. In ways that are playful and sometimes mischievous, he uses rhyme to reshape words themselves—taking two words that do not naturally rhyme and bending one of them, sometimes nearly to the breaking point, until it fits the other. For instance, on "Gold Digger," one of his biggest commercial hits to date, he rhymes the following names: "Serena," "Trina," "Jennifer." It's obvious which one of these doesn't belong, but Kanye makes "Jennifer" rhyme with the others by transforming it into "Gina-fa." The rhyme is forced to the point of not being forced at all. Quite the opposite, it appears by design, just another way to do something with language. Here's another example from Kanye's "Can't Tell Me Nothing" (2007):

Don't ever fix your lips like collagen
To say something when you're gon' end up apolagin'

"Collagen" is a word with absolutely no perfect rhymes. Rather than avoid the word entirely, Kanye instead uses the word's intractability to rhyme as a tool to reshape another word. We immediately understand what he means when he says "apolagin'," so he has not sacrificed meaning. Or take this rhyme from "Barry Bonds": "I don't need writers I might bounce ideas." He somehow makes "writers" rhyme with "ideas" by transforming the former into "wry-tears." What he has done in each of these cases is distorted sound for the sake of style, the poetic equivalent of Jimi Hendrix using his amp's feedback in his solo. Certainly many other artists have forced words to rhyme—often awkwardly, in a desperate attempt to make it fit—but few have forced them with such purpose and such measured understanding of the desired effect.

Where MCs rhyme their words has become just as important to rap's poetics as how they rhyme them. Rap is often presumed to rely heavily upon rhyming couplets. Most rap parodies are nothing more than a series of rigid couplets. But real MCs are rarely bounded by such limitations. While end rhymes, and particularly couplets, remain the foundation of rap's rhyme scheme, they are far from the only rhyme scheme in rap.

Over the years rap has undergone an internal rhyme revolution. Internal rhymes broaden rap's expressive range, enabling MCs to satisfy their listeners' lust for rhyme even as they claim greater freedom of motion to express complex ideas beyond the bounds of end rhyme. Unlike literary poets, who also wished to liberate themselves from the restrictions of end rhyme, MCs have done so while still satisfying their audience's desire for lines rich in rhyme. The explanation for this lies in rap's orality. Because rap is meant to be heard rather than read, it matters less where exactly the rhymes fall in the line. Two rhymes in the same line, while not the same as two lines with end rhymes, still have a pleasing effect on the ear. Notice how Posdnuos from De La Soul uses this technique on "The Bizness":

> While others **EXPLORE** to make it **HARDCORE**
> I make it **HARD FOR** wack MCs to even step in**SIDE THE DOOR**
> 'Cause these kids is **RHYMING, SOME-TIMING**
> And when we get to racing on the mic, they line up to see
> The lyrical **KILLING**, with stained egos on the **CEILING**

He begins with four rhymes in the first two lines, follows that with an internal rhyme in the third, no rhyme in the fourth, returning to an internal rhyme in the fifth. You would not have been likely to find that unrhymed line in rap's early years. Andre 3000 is a master of using internal rhymes to create opportunities for unrhymed lines, often eschewing end rhymes for a complex pattern of internal ones. Consider these lines from his guest verse on the R&B singer Lloyd's 2007 song "I Want You (Remix)":

> I said, "What time you get off?" She said,
> "When you get me off." I kinda laughed but it turned into
>   a cough
> 'Cause I swallowed down the wrong pipe.
> Whatever that mean, you know old people say it so it
>   sounds right.

These four lines include no end rhymes, and yet they more than satisfy our desire for rhyme. He achieves this by including internal rhyme, a phonic echo that fuses lines one and two ("off," "off," "cough").

Heading in the direction opposite to that of MCs like Andre 3000, who often eschew end rhyme entirely, a host of MCs have embraced a rhyme style that extends the repetition of a particular rhyme sound even beyond the couplet. Embracing the restriction of rhyme repetition, they seek to accentuate rhyme's pure effect. Many southern rappers, from Gorilla Zoe to Plies, follow this model. It would be a mistake to dismiss their styles as pedestrian. Instead, it might be useful to interpret them as aspiring to a different aesthetic from those MCs with more complicated rhyme styles. The fact that Jeezy, for instance, ends every line of "I Luv It" with a straightforward rhyme doesn't get in the way of his rhyme style, it *defines* it.

We might think of these extended end-rhyme riffs as links that form a rhyme chain. *Chain rhyme* is a technique whereby a poet carries a single rhyme over a succession of lines. The effect is often incantatory, lulling the listener into an almost trancelike state. Rhyme takes on a kind of rhythmic function here, underscoring specific patterns of sound to achieve its desired effect. While chain rhyming is now common in rap, rap was certainly not the first genre to use it. We can trace chain rhyming at least as far back as the fifteenth-century English poet John Skelton, who composed these lines:

> Tell you I chyll,
> If that ye wyll
> A whyle be styll,
> Of a comely gyll
> That dwelt on a hyll:

But she is not gryll,
For she is somewhat sage
And well worne in age;
For her visage
It would aswage
A mannes courage.

Skelton's lines consist of two and sometimes three stressed syllables connected by rhyme "leashes"—extended runs of the same end rhyme. The style is known as Skeltonics. In the above example, Skelton rhymes six short lines with "yll" and another five with "age," creating bursts of sound, a quickened pace, and an aggressive assertion of pattern. It comes as little surprise, then, that Skelton often used such a style when delivering, as he does in the above example, comic insults. Like a fifteenth-century battle rapper, Skelton uses rhyme chains to underscore his energy, aggression, and—to use a very twenty-first-century word for it—swagger.

Fast forward from Skelton to the present day and we can witness numerous hip-hop artists extending the spirit, if not the explicit form, of his rhyme style. While the nature of rap beats won't allow for Skeltonics' strict adherence to two- and three-syllable lines, it leaves ample room for chain rhyming.

Among the increasing number of rappers who use the chain-rhyming style is Fabolous. Since his debut in 2001, Fab has been known for delivering two distinct and even contradictory themes in his rhymes: crafty punch-line disses and plaintive love laments. Regardless of the theme, however, he employs the same rhyme-rich style. On his 2001 hit "Trade It All" he spits these lines in chain rhyme:

> You're the one, baby girl, I've never been so **SURE**
> Your skin's so **PURE**, the type men go **FOR**
> The type I drive the Benz slow **FOR**
> The type I be beepin' the horn, rollin' down the windows **FOR**

Using identity (the repetition of the same end word in successive lines, like "for" and "for"), and rhyming internally as well as at the end of his lines, Fabolous delivers a verse dominated by the ebb and flow of his repetition. Such repetition is the hallmark of his style, as we can see when comparing the above lines to his more recent hit, 2007's "Baby Don't Go":

> Through the time I been **ALONE**, time I spent on **PHONES**
> Know you ain't lettin them climb up in my **THRONE**
> Now, baby, that lime with that **PATRÓN**
> Have me talkin' crazy, it's time to come on **HOME**
> Now, I talk with someone **ABOVE**
> It's okay to lose your **PRIDE** over someone you **LOVE**
> Don't lose someone you **LOVE** though over your **PRIDE**
> Stick wit'cha entree and get over your **SIDE**

Like "Trade It All," "Baby Don't Go" is dominated by Fab's run of rhymes. But his style seems to show some development in the direction of variety and versatility. Instead of rhyming on a single sound, he weaves together three distinct rhymes, interlacing the last two ("pride" and "love") through chiasmus (a rhetorical figure in which two clauses are related to each other through reversal of structure or terms). The rhythmic effect is just as strong as it was in the earlier example, but he has added to it a more varied range of poetic effects, of thought as well as sound. Rap poetics as a whole has undergone a similar rhyme expansion and built upon its foundation to explore novel innovations in sound.

The way rappers rhyme has changed dramatically over time. Part of why old-school rap sounds old to our ears when compared to more recent rhymes is that it tends to employ simple end rhymes. The difference between the sound of old-school and new-school rap is largely attributable to the delivery and the position of the rhymes. Old-school rappers tended to employ end-stopped lines with rhymes falling at the end of lines, often in couplets. Their styles generally sound more effusive, dramatic, and artificial. Today you are more likely to hear conversational flows and natural rhymes, both internal and end rhymes, delivered in something closer to the rapper's natural voice. Rap rhymes in recent years have increased in variety and frequency. Layered patterns of internal rhymes and rhyme chains are now as important as end-rhymed lines.

To say that rap has developed, however, is not always to say it has improved. No rapper has ever improved upon the best rhymes of Rakim, or KRS-One, or Melle Mel. Distinguishing the ways rap's poetics have expanded in the years since these great MCs first recorded is not to discredit them, but rather to celebrate them anew for fashioning excellence with fewer poetic tools from which to choose.

Rap's rhyme revolution has not come in degrees, but in fits and starts—individual artists introducing new ways of rhyming, often going against the established practices of the era. Rap's development has also been responsive, new rhymes born to fit the increasingly complex and melodic rhythms in its instrumental production. New beats demand new rhymes.

The earliest rhymes in rap were basic, improvised, almost coincidental, recalls Grandmaster Caz of the Cold Crush Brothers, one of hip hop's originators. "When I started out as a DJ, MC-in' as an art hadn't been formulated yet," he says. "The microphone was just used for makin' announcements, like when the next party was gonna be, or people's moms would come to the party lookin' for them." The MC was born out of necessity. Caz's description of how he came to rhyme reads something like a rap creation story:

> So different DJs started embellishing what they were sayin'. Instead of just sayin', "We'll be at the P.A.L. next week, October this and that," they'd say, "You know next week we gonna be at the P.A.L. where we rock well, and we want to see your face in the place," little things like that. . . . I would make an announcement this way, and somebody would hear me, and then they'd go to their party and they add a little twist to it. Then somebody would hear that and they add a little bit to it. I'd hear it again and take it a little step further 'til it turned from lines to sentences to paragraphs to verses to rhymes.

Somewhere in that space between lines and rhymes, rap was born. Caz himself would prove one of the pivotal figures in rap's development. It was Caz's book of rhymes that ended up in the hands of a pizzeria employee by the name of Henry Jackson, aka Big Bank Hank, and it would be Caz's rhymes that would soon appear in Hank's verse from rap's first mainstream hit, "Rapper's Delight." Caz would never receive compensation.

But his influence, and that of rap's other MC pioneers—Coke La Rock, Clark Kent, Cowboy, Melle Mel, and others—would shape the structure of rap's poetics. Rap's first several years were dominated by the DJ; even the first rhymes were delivered from behind the turntables. In the late 1970s, however, the MC began to emerge as a coequal partner in hip-hop music. Around the same time, rap's center of gravity began its gradual move from clubs, basements, and block parties to the recording studio.

Rhyme, and the music it makes, has always had a cherished place in African-American expressive culture. From the ring shouts of the slaves to the singsong rhymes of children playing double dutch, from the verbal duels of the dozens to the ribald toasts told in barbershops and on street corners, black voices have found in rhyme a potent means of recreation and release. Muhammad Ali reveled in rhyme; a recent book, simply called *Ali Rap*, even called him "the first heavyweight champion of rap." But never before in black oral culture had an art form so relied upon rhyme to define itself. Rap takes rhyme farther than it had ever gone before.

The first rap song to hit the charts was "King Tim III (Personality Jock)" by the funk-disco collective the Fatback Band; it was released in late 1979, just before the Sugar Hill Gang officially inaugurated hip hop's commercial arrival with "Rapper's Delight." Listening to these songs now, in the era of lyrical wordsmiths like Andre 3000, Jay-Z, and Lil Wayne, it's a wonder that all of this music can go by the same name, so different is the oldest of the old-school from the new-school lyrics of today. The rhymes in "King Tim III" have a kind of innocent simplicity to them, a directness and predictability that sounds quaint to an ear attuned to slant rhymes and layered patterns of rhyming words. To understand the revolutionary nature of "King Tim III" and "Rapper's Delight" one must imagine a time when, save for a

select group of young New Yorkers, no one had ever heard
a voice doing what these voices were doing to the beat.

> Just clap your hands and stomp your feet
> 'Cause you're listenin' to the sound of the sure-shot beat
> K-I-N-G the T-I-M
> King Tim the third and I am him
> Just me, Fatback, and the groove
> Are doing it all just for you
> Strong as an ox and tall as a tree
> I can rock it so viciously

The rhymes are simple, monosyllabic, and mostly perfect, rhymed in playful couplets that settle comfortably into
the pocket of the beat. The tone is lighthearted, befitting a
party spirit. These are good-times rhymes, uncomplicated by
image or wordplay. And yet they embody a rhyme revolution; no other musical genre would so foreground the effects
of language itself, its sound as well as its meaning. No other
music would demand to be understood as both speech and
song, poetry and music all at once.

This first generation of MCs made up the rules as it went
along. By necessity, they drew from every source available to
inform the way they put their words together. The rhymes
nearest at hand were often those for advertising jingles or play-
ground chants, even nursery rhymes. The language they fashioned was at once innovative and traditional.

That lines like King Tim's—so contrived, so simplistic to
us today—were not only accepted but celebrated shows just
how new the form actually was. By the 1970s, mainstream
literary poets had mostly cut themselves off from rhyme,

especially end rhyme. The few sources where one could still hear it were often aimed at children. Rap stepped in to fill a cultural void, to provide the pleasure of rhyme in terms that adults could appreciate.

One MC above all others is responsible for consolidating and codifying the dominant rhyme style of the old school: Melle Mel. As mentioned before, Melle Mel emerged as perhaps the most talented MC of his era. As part of Grandmaster Flash and the Furious Four (later the Furious Five), he pioneered, along with his brother Kid Creole, Cowboy, and Scorpio, the modern style of the MC. Beginning with "Superrappin'" in 1979 and continuing through a range of hip-hop classics like "The Message," "White Lines," "Beat Street," and more, Melle Mel stands as the dominant poetic voice of rap's early years.

Melle Mel's rhyme style began rather humbly. Kid Creole explains it like this: "When we first started rhyming, Flash would have guys on the microphone who'd just get on there and say his name, haphazard, no real talent being displayed. And my brother . . . I don't know, somehow or another he got in his head that he was going to try to make up his own rhymes, and that's what he did." The style of rhyming Melle Mel developed relied upon both regularity and occasional surprise. His verses establish patterns of end and internal rhymes, fusing both sonically and thematically his lines into verses. This method is in evidence in the opening bars from "White Lines (Don't Do It)":

> Ticket to ride, white-line **HIGHWAY**
> Tell all your friends, they can go **MY WAY**
> Pay your **TOLL**, sell your **SOUL**

Pound for pound costs more than **GOLD**
The longer you **STAY** the more you **PAY**
My white lines go a long **WAY**
Either up your nose or through your **VEIN**
With nothing to **GAIN** except killin' your **BRAIN**

Melle Mel begins the verse with a compound multisyllabic broken rhyme ("highway" and "my way"), then follows it up with three sets of couplets, each containing three rhymes on the same sound—two end and one internal. The result is a verse rich in rhyme and textured in sound.

In the years since Melle Mel and rap's other rhyme innovators, MCs have refined a range of rhyme techniques, extending both the rap tradition and the poetic tradition as a whole. Rap started a revolution of sense as well as sound, expanding the capacity of language to express the human experience in all its diversity.

THREE Wordplay

YEARS AGO A friend of mine asked me to defend rap. We were driving back to campus after a basketball game, and I was playing a new disc for her, *Ready to Die*, from an emerging Brooklyn rapper named the Notorious B.I.G. It was just beginning to dawn on me, as it was on many hip-hop heads, that we were witnessing lyrical greatness with Biggie. By late 1994 he was a star, by 1995 he was an icon, and by his untimely death in 1997 he was a legend. Some still consider him the most skilled lyricist of all time. Almost everyone ranks him among the most influential MCs in hip-hop history. In that moment, however, I was dealing with something more tangible: the capacity of words—specific words—to do harm.

"Why do you like this, Adam? I expect more from you," my friend said, as we idled at a stoplight listening to the percussive assault of "Machine Gun Funk." Her eyes demanded a response.

For a moment I was silent. I knew she was talking about Biggie's almost manic repetition of "nigga" and "bitch," not to mention his offhanded use of garden-variety curse words—"shit," "damn," "muthafucka." Biggie wasn't helping my case very much, either, rhyming this profane but indelible simile just as I was about to speak: "That's why I pack a nina, fuck a misdemeanor / beating muthafuckas like Ike beat Tina." When I finally responded, I had a hard time even convincing myself.

"It's not what he's saying, it's how he's saying it," I said. "And, besides, they're just words!"

Just words. It is rap's perennial problem. Most hip-hop fans find themselves at one time or another in the position of defending the indefensible, of making the case to excuse the coarse language and the misogynistic messages behind some of rap's best-known lyrics. Such instances of offense present a particular problem for a book that advocates reading rap lyrics on the page as poetry. Things that might escape attention in performance become all the more explicit when viewed in black-and-white in an MC's book of rhymes.

So in some ways I find myself today in the same position I found myself in more than a decade ago while listening to Biggie. How do you explain without apologizing? How do you resist without rejecting? To understand hip hop as a cultural movement we must explore the roots and the reasons for its explicit nature. Rap often specifically intends to offend polite sensibilities. After all, it is an art form born on the street corner, speaking a language of the corner as well. It has evolved, to borrow hip-hop historian William Jelani Cobb's phrase, from the "shunned expressions of disposable people." In that way, it is no different from a host of earlier expressive traditions that came from the bottom of the social spectrum. "Each poet creates his own language from that which he finds around him," Ralph Ellison explained to an interviewer in 1958, speaking about the distinctive language of black American poets. "Thus if these [vernacular] poets find the language of Shakespeare or Racine inadequate to reach their own peoples, then the other choice is to re-create their original language to the point where they may express their complex emotions." Hip hop's first generation did exactly this, forging a language responsive to the needs of its creators, reflecting their own complex emotions.

Rap's revolutionary spirit lies in the force of necessity behind so much of its expression. "When I was young," recalls the pioneering female rapper MC Lyte, "I was like, how else can a young black girl of my age be heard all around the world? I gotta rap." The rapper Common echoes Lyte's assertion of rap's necessity. "Hip hop has so much power," he explains. "The government can't stop it. The devil can't stop it. It's music, it's art, it's the voice of the people. And it's being spoken all around the world and the world is appreciating it. And it is helping to change things. . . . It's definitely uplifting the ghetto and giving the ghetto a chance for its voice to be heard."

Rap's profanity at least in part responds to this unmet need. Harsh words are sometimes required to describe harsh realities. Again, Ellison is instructive. "The great body of Negro slang—that unorthodox language—exists precisely because Negroes need words which will communicate, which will designate the objects, processes, manners and subtleties of their urban experience with the least amount of distortion from the outside," Ellison wrote. He was describing school-children in 1950s Harlem, but he might as well have been writing about rappers. The origins of rap as an artistic protest partly explain rap's continuing profanity.

Equally important is rap's identity as an outlaw expression, a form that doesn't mind using the words that people actually say, words that describe the sometimes unseemly reality of our modern life. "A language comes into existence by means of brutal necessity, and the rules of the language are dictated by what the language must convey," James Baldwin wrote in an editorial for the *New York Times* entitled "If Black English Isn't a Language, Then Tell Me, What Is?" published in 1979, just around the time of rap's public emergence. Baldwin saw in black English in general what he might have seen in rap in particular, the workings of a vital new form of linguistic expression.

Raekwon of the Wu-Tang Clan suggests Baldwin's understanding of language's birth in brutal necessity when offering this profound—and profane—reflection upon rap's explicit, poetic language. "People may look at it like, 'Some of them talk about violence,' whatever—but first say the nigga's a poet," he says. "To flow—that shit is not easy. You can never get it no fresher, comin' up out of the projects, twenty years old, and you start rhymin', and that's how you make your money—by speaking your lingo. Rap, to me, is slang poetry. It answers your questions: why young kids is doin' bad, why they turn to drugs to get away from their misery. This is the shit we talk about—and how to escape it." Any language with such salvific power must not be ignored.

There is no defense for the sexism, homophobia, and violence found in certain rap lyrics. These elements remain a troubling reality of rap's expression, and a part—one must unfortunately add—of a larger culture that sanctions such beliefs in ways both big and small.

But rap at its best retains meaning that extends well beyond its sometimes offensive surface. It is a complex linguistic art where words are constantly in flux, changing meanings and intentions, texture and sound. The Romantic poet Percy Bysshe Shelley argued that the primary function of figurative language was to render the familiar unfamiliar. In other words, similes and metaphors have the capacity to reshape our vision of the world. More than any other contemporary form of linguistic expression, rap plays with words in ways that jar us from our settled sense of reality, opening up new ways of seeing and even feeling. This, too, makes it poetry.

Our culture, however, usually treats rap as if it were transparent, as if its poetry were nothing more than the clear cellophane wrapper around its "literal" meaning. Both rap's greatest advocates and its loudest detractors each tend to interpret rap as direct speech. For many of its fans, rap is the word from the street, or as Chuck D is said to have remarked, it is CNN for black people. For its critics, rap is a megaphone spewing hate speech, a purveyor of violence, sexism, and homophobia. These opposing extremes each contain a certain truth: rap has undoubtedly given voice to those who might not otherwise have been heard; at the same time, it has helped popularize the flagrant denigration of women and gays in the broader culture. These tensions remain unresolved in rap culture.

One might be tempted to ask, as CNN did in a 2007 special report: "Hip-Hop: Art or Poison?" But this is a false choice. To focus solely on rap's perceived ends, whether beneficial or toxic, is to misunderstand the central role of its expressive *means*. Rap cannot be distilled into pure meaning. No matter how profound or offensive or funny rappers' messages may be, their words are inextricably bound up in the way that MCs deliver them: through rhythm, rhyme, imagery, tone of voice. "Rather than being *about* experience, think of a poem *as* an experience—sometimes with memorable insights, sometimes not." So explains the poet Frances Mayes in words that seem particularly relevant to rap. To define rap as poetry is not necessarily to defend it as always good for us. But a mature audience can understand rap in context and measure its value not simply in the quantity of its curse words, but in the variety and sophistication of its poetic forms.

Like all poetry, rap is necessarily communication. It relies upon repetition and artful departures from that repetition, both in its percussive instrumentals and in its rhythm- and rhyme-rich lyrics. It fashions itself as a ritualized language, heightening sound, establishing patterns of expectation and innovation, and crafting images that engage the audience in an implicit but powerful process of communication. "It's just a vehicle," explains the West Coast rhymer Ras Kass, "At its purest form, that's what hip hop is. It's communication."

The way rap communicates is what makes it such a powerful poetic form. Rap does what the poet Edward Hirsch claims the lyric poem does: it "defamiliarizes words, it wrenches them from familiar or habitual contexts, it puts a spell on them." It does all of this with rhythm, rhyme, and

wordplay. As we have seen, rhythm establishes aural relations among words that one does not find in conventional
speech and rhyme compels the MC to conceive connections
between previously disconnected words and ideas. For all the
controversy about rap's use of profanity, a simple truth remains: Rap is finally less about those words whose meanings
are obvious and more about those words whose meanings are
not readily apparent.

"That's the part of hip-hop that's missing," says Pusha T,
one-half of the Clipse, bemoaning what he sees as the dimin-
ishing importance of wordplay in today's hip hop. For a group
known for their gritty tales of the drug game, wordplay might
seem the furthest thing from their minds. In fact, the opposite is the case. Wordplay matters to them because it enables
them to create art that transcends their subject matter, the
so-called cocaine rap for which they're known. "It's one
thing to say 'I sell bricks, I sell bricks,'" he continues, "But
when you saying 'Trunk like Aspen / Looking like a million
muthafuckin' crushed aspirins,' dog, we getting back to the
colors. A lot of dudes is working with the eight crayons in
the box. They do not have the sixty-four box, yo. They don't
got 'Burnt Sienna.' They got red, yellow, blue. . . . " Wordplay gives color and texture to rap's poetry, allowing
MCs to craft subtle shades of meaning and feeling instead
of paint-by-numbers lines. Wordplay creates possibility out of
limitation.

Wordplay may be the most revolutionary way that rap refash-
ions the language. Rap's wordplay creates surprising figures of
speech and thought that bind words and ideas in unexpected
ways. Few would ever listen to someone talking over a beat,

and yet millions listen to MCs rapping over one. Understanding this difference has important implications for rap, both as a poetic form and as a cultural phenomenon. Wordplay is the common term to describe the array of techniques MCs have developed over the years to do things with words. These include everything from common figures like simile and metaphor to more obscure figures like chiasmus and antanaclasis. Whether transferring, exchanging, or transforming meaning from one word to another, the figures and forms of rap wordplay comprise the most varied element of rap's poetics.

Rap's wordplay comes in dozens of varieties, each with an explicit function in language and thought. Together they serve an essential purpose for the rap poet, empowering them to fashion new connections between familiar words and ideas. "All poetry implies the destruction of the relationship between things that seems obvious to us in favor of particular relationships imposed by the poet," writes André Malraux. MCs do precisely this by rendering the familiar unfamiliar, and thus defining attitudes and emotions in ways that more direct speech cannot. Whether they explain or obscure, pattern or disrupt, the best MCs play with language to create unexpected moments of insight and feeling. Common put it best when he rhymed, "My imagery talks, metaphors and similes stalk."

Rap defines itself as something other, something more, than conventional speech. Like other art forms, it tailors the world to fit its own conception. As a result, rap relies upon adornment, with figurative language being hip hop's lyrical haute couture. As Kool G Rap once rhymed, using an extended metaphor, "Lyrics are fabrics, beat is the lining / My passion for rhyming is fashion designing." Consider the simile the most accessible and versatile way that MCs can dress up their words.

A *simile* is a direct comparison between two distinctly different things, usually using *like* or *as* to connect them. In their simplest form, similes offer direct comparisons for the purpose of revealing the unexpected similarity of disparate things. William Shakespeare's sonnet 60 begins with this simile: "Like as the waves make toward the pebbled shore / so do our minutes hasten to their end." In these two lines he asks us to reimagine time as something other than a clock on the wall; through simile, time instead becomes the continuous sequence of waves that break against the shore. Andre 3000 boasting that he's "cooler than a polar bear's toenails" turns the simile to yet another purpose, using a completely unexpected comparison to define his state of being. Both show the power of figurative language to remake the ordinary into the extraordinary.

Similes, though they are often confused with metaphors, are the most common figure of speech in rap. By contrast, a *metaphor* is when one thing is said to *be* another without the use of *like* or *as*. Shakespeare composed a famous one when he wrote these lines in *As You Like It*: "All the world's a stage / And all the men and women merely players." By making positive assertions of identity (the world *is* a stage, not like a stage), metaphors ask us to make a direct connection between two distinct things. Both metaphor and simile work on the same principle: They transfer meaning from one thing to another. The only difference is the means of that transfer— the vehicle, if you will. Think of the metaphor as the express train on the subway: It gets you between two points fast using the most direct route. The simile can be thought of as the bus: It takes its sweet time getting you from one place to another, and leaves you free to look out the window to see exactly how you got where you're going.

The difference between simile and metaphor is not merely technical. After all, there has to be some reason why similes so outnumber metaphors in rap. My hypothesis is this: Metaphor is a more implicit form, thus leaving itself open to misunderstanding and potentially detracting from its subject—which is usually the "I" of the MC. When Nas boasts that "I'm like a whole lotta loot, I'm like new money," the simile underscores his greatness. If he'd rhymed instead, "I'm a whole lot of loot, I'm new money," our first response would likely be, "What does that mean?" The last thing an MC wants to do with wordplay is cause confusion. Similes shine the spotlight on their subject more directly than do metaphors. They announce their artifice from the beginning, leaving little room for confusion. On a more practical note, similes are more immediately comprehensible to listeners, a virtue in rap's rapid-fire lyricism.

Not all similes, however, are created equal. Rap offers a variety unrivaled in contemporary literature. The two rap similes I quote on the next page demonstrate the range of potential difference. The first is a classic old-school example from Rakim. The second comes from Souls of Mischief's Tajai, recorded during rap's golden age in the early 1990s. Of course, this comparison is no reflection on the relative skill of these two MCs—this isn't a battle—but it will, I hope, demonstrate just how rap similes are made and how they can differ from one another. First, here are a few lines from Rakim's classic "I Ain't No Joke" (the simile is in bold, and I've provided a few extra lines for context):

I GOT A QUESTION, IT'S SERIOUS AS CANCER:
Who can keep the average rap dancer
hyper as a heart attack, nobody smiling,
'cause you're expressing the rhyme that I'm styling.

Every simile contains one thing that is being compared
to another: The item being compared, in this case Rakim's
"question," is known as the *tenor*. The item to which the
tenor is compared (here it's "cancer") is known as the *vehicle*
because it delivers meaning to the tenor—it's the "bus," to
use my previous analogy. Normally, similes are comparisons
between the same parts of speech (nouns to nouns, verbs to
verbs). In this example, we have two nouns, and the vehicle
is loaded with the adjective "serious." Here, then, is how
Rakim's simile works in our minds: Cancer is a serious
ailment—it's a leading cause of death in the United States—
so Rakim's question must be serious too, because it borrows
its gravity from the disease. Notably, Rakim chooses not to
use the more commonplace—and cliché—"serious as a heart
attack"; by using a new and unfamiliar comparison, he makes
his simile that much more powerful.

Sometimes rap similes compare not what something is
like but how something is done, as with Tajai's simile from
"Disseshowedo":

In battles I rip it and it gets hectic after
I FLIP THE SCRIPT LIKE A DYSLEXIC ACTOR
You're no factor . . .

The tenor is "I" and the vehicle is "dyslexic actor." The
vehicle is loaded with a verb—really a verbal phrase—"flip
the script." This is a slightly more ambitious simile than

Rakim's because it functions with a double meaning: *Flipping the script* is a popular phrase that can mean "changing up the subject matter," and one need not explain how an actor with dyslexia might jumble up his lines. The meaning communicated here is as much about the cleverness of the wordplay as it is about the force of the simile itself. The simile's expressive function stops when it has communicated its meaning; in this instance, when it communicates that Tajai flips the script in the sense that a dyslexic actor would. But the real richness of the wordplay is mostly conveyed in the unexpected wit of Tajai's punning comparison.

Conventionally understood, the most effective similes are those that ask us to conceive connections between words that seem far removed from one another. The simile at once reveals hidden similarities even as it affirms obvious differences; both elements are essential for the simile to work.

Most rap similes follow the model of Tajai, where not only is one thing "like" another, but the thing to which something is compared also has a double meaning. This is commonly achieved by combining similes with puns. *Puns* thrive in the ambiguity of meaning that similes create. They play on the different senses of the same word and the similar senses of different ones. Puns often serve as coded forms of communication, speaking to a select group of initiates with a shared set of cultural knowledge and assumptions. At their most obscure, they can act as inside jokes intended for a relative few; these are invisible to the average reader or listener. At their broadest, they are immediately discernable to nearly everyone, in which case they demand little of the audience and offer little in return. But there is a middle ground between the obscure and the obvious in which the pun has the capacity to do something to language and demand something of the audience. In poetry where a premium is put upon verbal economy, any technique that has the capacity of expanding the meaning of a single word is valuable. When artfully rendered, puns do just that: opening a range of associations that the poet/MC can exploit for the purposes of original expression.

In the literary tradition, puns have often been derided as an inferior species of expression, good for little more than a cheap laugh. And yet the world's greatest literature employs them for a host of purposes, from the comic to the tragic and even to the sacred. The Bible itself is not above the pun. Matthew 16:18 reads, "Thou art Peter, and upon this rock I will build my church." This is a pun in the Greek source upon "Peter" (*Petros*) and "rock" (*petra*), homonyms for stone. To the initiate, puns have a sophisticated range of uses, well beyond the limits of humor.

Puns have an important place in the Western poetic heritage as well. Shakespeare used puns throughout his plays and sonnets, often for the purpose of blunt sexual humor. The very title of his great comedy *Much Ado About Nothing* turns a pun on its last word, which was slang in Elizabethan times for vagina. One of Shakespeare's contemporaries, the poet John Donne, also explored the expressive capacity of puns. *A Hymn to God the Father* puns on Donne's last name, as well as the last name of his wife, Ann More: "When Thou has done, Thou hast not done, / For I have more." Similarly, in *A Valediction: Forbidding Mourning* Donne crafts an extended pun that plays upon sex for a second level of meaning. These are meanings above and beyond the functional meanings of the lines as read on the surface.

Puns elicit an equal range of responses in rap. When well executed, they announce the MC's lyrical virtuosity and cognitive ingenuity. When combined with similes, puns become a powerful expressive tool for the rap poet. Conventional similes, as discussed earlier, rely upon the transfer of meaning from one thing to another. If I say, "I'm cold as ice," the essence of ice's coldness is transferred to me. When rappers add puns to their similes, the possible number of transferable meanings increases exponentially. So instead of saying, "I'm cold as ice," Lil Wayne says something like this: "And I'm so cold like Keisha's family." Read as a conventional simile, the statement is nonsensical. Read as simile-pun hybrid, it comes alive. The simile awakens our comprehension of the pun, and visa versa. This figure relies upon the fact that Lil Wayne pronounces "cold" like "coal," or rather, like "Cole," the surname of the R&B singer Keisha Cole. For the simile to function, we must first catch the pun on the family name, then reflect the strength of the comparison (Cole equals Keisha's family) back upon Lil Wayne himself (his style is just as cold as Keisha's family is Cole). This is a poetic freedom rappers didn't inherit; they created it for themselves out of the need for expressive range and the desire for verbal ingenuity.

Punning similes are now the norm in rap, displaying a versatility of tone and intention from the comic to the serious. When Juelz Santana drops this line on "I Am Crack," he's not cracking a joke, he's flexing his mic skills: "I'm more amazing than Grace is when I say shit / You should say 'Amen' after my name, kid." Kanye West, however, delivers this punning simile from "The Good Life" with a wink and a smile: "The good life, so keep it comin' with the bottles / 'Til she feel booze like she bombed at Apollo." This bit of wordplay relies upon the pun on "booze/boos," the kind you drink and the kind that lets you know when it's time to leave the stage. The simile only makes sense after we've made the mental adjustment to the double meaning, and it is complete only after we reinterpret the first part of the simile in light of the second. Those crowds at Harlem's Apollo Theatre are notorious for booing poor performers off stage (they even booed a young Luther Vandross), so we know through the simile that Kanye's female companion is in for quite a hangover.

Most rappers use similes to convey meaning from one thing to another. This is a simple enough thing to do. Rap's recognized masters of wordplay distinguish themselves by crafting inventive comparisons and surprising turns of phrase. Some are comedians, using similes to deliver punch lines. Others are more self-consciously dramatic, underscoring meaning with similes that force us to consider two unlikely subjects in the same terms. In other words, while all similes follow the same basic structure, the meanings they create can range from the witty to the whimsical, the sorrowful to the sublime.

One MC who has earned a reputation for his highly crafted similes and metaphors is Immortal Technique. His rhymes are densely layered with figurative language, particularly punning similes. They serve both as weapons and as wake-up calls to jar his listeners to attention. One of the best examples of his wordplay in action is the opening eight bars of "Industrial Revolution." His lyrics offer a series of examples that display a multiplicity of effective similes in action.

The bling-bling era was cute but it's about to be done,
I leave you full of clips like the moon blockin' the sun.
My metaphors are dirty like herpes but harder to catch.
Like an escape tunnel in prison, I started from scratch
And now these parasites want a piece of my ASCAP,
trying to control perspective like an acid flashback;
but here's a quotable for every single record exec:
Get your fuckin' hands out my pocket, nigga, like Malcolm X.

These lines include five similes, each structured in a different way from the next. The first, "I leave you full of clips like the moon blockin' the sun," relies on oral expression—when he raps the line "full of clips" it also sounds like "full eclipse." It shows the range of possibility open to an MC that is closed for the most part to a literary poet. Another complex simile is "like an escape tunnel in prison, I started from scratch." In this case, "I" is the tenor and "escape tunnel in prison" is the vehicle. The vehicle transfers the phrase "started from scratch," which has a dual meaning—both literal and figurative. We hear it as both "starting with nothing but the raw materials" and as "starting by scratching away at a wall placed squarely in your way." By literalizing this common—even cliché—figure of speech, Immortal Technique creates an unusually potent simile.

Finally, the last line, "Get your fuckin' hands out my pocket, nigga, like Malcolm X," demonstrates some of the ambiguities in interpreting similes. The overall meaning of what he's saying couldn't be any clearer: record executives need to stop taking money away from him for his music. However, the simile isn't nearly as clear. For one, it doesn't respond well to the way we've been breaking the previous similes down. What is the tenor? "Your hands"? And the vehicle? Certainly it's "Malcolm X," but does he mean the man or the Spike Lee film? (The line that follows—"but this ain't a movie"—favors the latter.) Whatever the vehicle, the meaning it conveys is "Get your hands out my pocket," the phrase that one of Malcolm X's assassins yelled to cause a distraction when Malcolm was gunned down on February 21, 1965, while speaking at the Audubon Ballroom. However, this only makes sense with the movie in a general way; that line, or its near equivalent, is in the film. Suffice it to say that this simile, though it doesn't quite work in the strict formal sense, nonetheless does the job, and does it well on the level of feeling. It is effective because it is emphatic, surprising, and historically grounded. Rap doesn't always play by the book.

Eminem is another master of the simile; he seems to revel in the ways that he can break and reshape the laws of the language. Unfortunately for those with sensitive ears, his rhymes must be considered required reading (not to mention listening) for anyone seriously interested in rap wordplay. One of the best examples of Eminem's creative expansion of simile comes from the opening lines of "The Real Slim Shady" where Eminem unleashes a single simile that takes up four full lines:

> Y'all act like you've never seen a white person before,
> jaws all on the floor like Pam, like Tommy just burst in the door
> and started whoopin' her ass worse than before
> they first were divorced, throwin' her over furniture . . .

The tenor and the vehicle, in this case, aren't simple nouns or verbs, but rather situations: the tenor being the shock of seeing a white person rapping, and the vehicle being the shock of seeing Tommy Lee abuse Pamela Anderson. The vehicle, then, is transporting the degree of shock (jaws on the floor) from the latter to the former. But what's so remarkable about the exchange is that while the tenor is implied in the first line, it is never explicitly stated. And the vehicle? It takes up twenty-two words and nearly three lines. By the end, you almost forget that he is using a simile at all. At that point, however, the simile has already done its work, communicating its meaning with dark humor.

Innovative MCs like Immortal Technique and Eminem have so expanded the simile that their lyrics barely resemble the basics discussed at the beginning of this chapter. In their rhymes, the line between simile and metaphor, though visible and significant, is never impermeable. Some MCs use similes with a kind of directness that comes closer to the effect commonly achieved by metaphors. A fine example of this can be found on a remarkable track from Andre 3000's *The Love Below*, "A Life in the Day of Benjamin Andre (Incomplete)." Andre rhymes without interruption for five full minutes, a rarity in recorded rap. The lines I've chosen come from a section describing the sexual exploits of life on the road.

> Girls used to say, "Y'all talk funny, y'all from the islands?"
> And I'd laugh and they'd just keep smilin'
> "No, I'm from Atlanta, baby. He from Savannah, maybe
> we should hook up and get tore up and then lay down—Hey, we
> gotta go because the bus is pullin' out in thirty minutes.
> She's playing tennis disturbing the tenants:

Fifteen-love, fit like glove.
**DESCRIPTION IS LIKE . . . FIFTEEN DOVES IN A JACUZZI
CATCHIN' THE HOLY GHOST
MAKIN' ONE WOOZY IN THE HEAD AND COMATOSE.** Agree?

Andre pauses right after "like" before completing the simile. The tenor, the "description" he seeks, is the description of sex, which he compares with the highly unusual vehicle "fifteen doves in a Jacuzzi catchin' the Holy Ghost." But what does the vehicle convey? Remarkably, nothing but itself. But in this case that is certainly enough. The "like" here, which helps identify this as a simile, seems almost extraneous. We experience this comparison unmediated by anything else. In this case, the simile really *is* a metaphor—or at least is acting like one.

Rap metaphors, though they are not nearly as common as you would expect given how often rappers mention the word itself in their rhymes, are nonetheless essential components of hip hop's figurative language. They have the benefit of directness and of self-conscious poetic artifice. In their simplest form, they positively assert that one thing *is* another, or at the very least that one thing is equal to another in some essential way. So when Kanye West boasts on "Swagger Like Us" that "my swagger is Mick Jagger," he's using metaphor to equate his confidence on the mic to the Rolling Stones' consummately cocky front man. For the instant it takes him to deliver that line, it's as if you've caught a glimpse of Mick himself strutting across the stage. Metaphors have that capacity to give the abstract concrete form.

In 1993's "Pink Cookies in a Plastic Bag," LL Cool J delivered perhaps one of rap's most unusual metaphors: "The act of making love is pink cookies in a plastic bag getting crushed by buildings." Like Andre in the example above, LL attempts to express the concrete act of lovemaking in the abstract terms of figurative language. Here the metaphor functions not so much to define as to obscure, obliterating tangible meaning (the "act of making love") by refashioning it in a series of incongruities (cookies, plastic bags, and buildings). This is but an extreme example of something that rappers do all the time with metaphor, extending meaning to just this side of the breaking point. It also illustrates the point I've been making about simile and metaphor's difference in form, but commonality in function. How would it change the expression, for instance, if LL had said instead that "the act of making love is *like* pink cookies in a plastic bag getting crushed by buildings"? It becomes somewhat less striking, more common, but it generally retains the essential effect of the comparison.

Metaphors lend themselves better than similes to certain types of abstract expression in rap. On "I Feel Like Dying," Lil Wayne offers up a series of metaphors to capture the drugged-out state of intoxication:

> I can mingle with the stars, and throw a party on Mars;
> I am a prisoner locked up behind Xanax bars.
> I have just boarded a plane without a pilot
> and violets are blue, roses are red
> daisies are yellow, the flowers are dead.
> Wish I could give you this feeling I feel like buying,
>   and if my dealer don't have no more, then (I feel
>   like dying).

As a metaphor for addiction, "I'm a prisoner locked up behind Xanax bars" is a powerful description, particularly given his pun on "bars": the name often used to refer to Xanax tablets and the bars of a prison cell. Weezy even resurrects and revitalizes the dead metaphors (those comparisons so overused that they retain little figurative impact) "roses are red, violets are blue" by recontextualizing them and capping them with the stark finality of "the flowers are dead." Capturing both the celestial highs and the morbid lows of his addiction, Lil Wayne's metaphors achieve an expressive power unattainable through conventional speech.

Rappers have occasionally employed metaphors in extended forms, often taking up the bulk of a verse or even an entire song. When metaphor does this, we understand it as a conceit. In literature a *conceit* is an extended metaphor that usually comprises the entirety of a poem. It asks the listener to consider a comparison between two things or two circumstances that might not immediately seem plausible. When combined with *personification*, endowing inanimate things with human traits, it can expand our understanding of the thing in question in ways that direct description could not.

Perhaps the MC with the most experiments in hip-hop personification to his name might be Nas. From the self-explanatory "Money Is My Bitch" to the more nuanced "I Gave You Power," where Nas raps in the first-person voice of a gun, he seems well aware of the expressive potential to be found in appealing to the human element in inanimate things. "I Gave You Power" is actually a species of personification known by its Greek name, *prosopopoeia*, a rhetorical device in which the poet writes from the perspective of another person or, in this case, object. By shifting the listener's perspective to that of a gun, Nas finds a way of speaking out against gun violence without being preachy. The song ends with the gun jamming, refusing to shoot at the victim: "He pulled the trigger but I held on, it felt wrong / He squeezed harder, I didn't budge, sick of the blood." Ultimately, though, the gun has limited control over its own fate. When its owner dies, shot by the person he meant to shoot, the gun finds itself in the hands of another.

Personification lends itself to such critiques. Rap's defining example of personification is undoubtedly Common's 1994 classic "I Used to Love H.E.R." The song works on two levels. On the literal level, it is Common's love story with a young girl he sees grow into womanhood, facing a host of challenges along the way. On the metaphorical level, it is the story of hip hop itself. Common asks us to see hip hop personified in the girl, and his love for hip hop, both lost and found, in his love for her. If we didn't grasp this metaphorical doubling on our own, Common makes sure that we get it. He gestures to the song's potential double meaning before he starts rhyming, simply in the acronym of the title (H.E.R.). Even if we have no idea what the acronym stands for (purportedly it is "Hip-Hop in its Essence and Real") we are tipped off that a double meaning, whatever it is, is there to be uncovered. If that weren't enough, his final line spells it out in no uncertain terms: "'Cause who I'm talking bout, y'all, is hip hop." What makes "I Used to Love H.E.R." work is that Common never overburdens his lyrics, on the narrative or the metaphorical level—indeed, it is possible to appreciate it simply as a love song without ever comprehending the conceit at work. Still, Common's doubling of meaning renders the song powerful on two levels, validating its reputation as one of the finest raps on wax.

Wordplay resides in such multiple meanings, even in the very names MCs choose to call themselves. Most rappers have aliases. You might not have heard of Dante Terrell Smith but you surely have heard of Mos Def. Dennis Coles is Ghostface Killah, sometimes just Ghostface, and also Iron Man or Tony Starks. This process of naming, of exchanging one identity for another, has found its way into the very language of rap lyricism. In general, rhetoricians classify such names as *epithets*, which literally means "imposed." A more specific variety of epithet is *kenning*, a trope that exchanges a given word or proper name for a compound poetic phrase. This style was first popularized in Old English poetry, largely forgotten, and now reborn today in rap. We can see kenning at work in rap precisely because it is the type of trope that elevates the speaker. So when Biggie rhymes "Teflon is the material for the imperial / mic-ripper, girl-stripper, the Henny-sipper," we see the MC rendering himself in epic proportions, and in the process reviving a figure of speech that peaked in popularity over a thousand years ago. The same holds true for these lines from Jean Grae's "Hater's Anthem," a vicious battle rap: "The cancer-toker, the Mad Hatter, the Jabberwocky of rap." Beginning with kenning, she moves to a more general form of epithet drawn from, of all things, Lewis Carroll's *Alice in Wonderland*.

Kenning is related to another important rhetorical figure in rap, the *eponym*, which in Greek means "named after." Rap eponyms usually appear when MCs exchange a particular attribute or action (in other words, an adjective or a verb) for a famous name that brings it to mind. This is a fairly rare figure, which makes it all the more surprising that Jay-Z has not one but three of them on a single song. On "Threats" from *The Black Album* he delivers the following eponyms:

> I'm especially Joe Pesci with it, friend
> I will kill you, commit suicide, and kill you again.
>
> We Rat Pack niggas, let Sam tap dance on you,
> then I Sinatra shot ya goddamn you.
>
> Y'all wish I was frontin', I George Bush the button.

Jay-Z's threats take the shape of eponyms invoking famous individuals who represent danger in the characters they portray (Pesci's ruthless Tommy DeVito from *Goodfellas*), the reputations that they carry (the Rat Pack with their reported links to the Mob), and the power they wield (Bush's presidential control over America's nuclear arsenal). Using eponyms instead of similes, Jay not only fashions more unusual—and fresh—figurative language, but also makes his meaning more powerful by enlisting his listeners' minds in making apparent the meaning of the lines.

Jay-Z returns to this same rhetorical figure on 2007's *American Gangster* album, combining it with another figure, *metonymy*—the use of one word to refer to something with which it is closely associated—to deliver the following clever line on "Party Life": "Your boy's off the wall, these other niggas is Tito." The line works because it engages the listener in a mental process of indirect and abstract communication. It asks us to make meaning out of context; our minds might not necessarily jump to Michael Jackson from the mention of "off the wall" alone, but with "Tito" too, Jay's line provides enough information for us to draw a strong inference. "Off the wall" is in a metonymic relationship with Michael Jackson because, as the title of his best early album, it is strongly associated with him. Tito works as an eponym because, unfair as it may be, his name is most often invoked to signal obscurity or failure. Just in case these meanings escape us, Jay glosses his own verse, speaking these lines over the hook: "Damn. Hey, baby, I said I'm off the wall, I'm like a young Michael Jackson, these other niggas is Tito. Shout out to Randy. Real talk!" It's a bravura gesture, a playful show of amazement at his own lyrical virtuosity. In its own way, it's also a kind of wordplay.

Metonymy's form of indirect but artful expression offers MCs new ways of saying familiar things. Few topics are more familiar to rap than the diss, which makes rhetorical figures like metonymy into a lyrical weapon. For instance, Nas uses metonymy in 2008's "Queens Get the Money" to deliver a coded diss at 50 Cent, who had suggested in an interview that Nas's rhyme skills had waned. Nas answers with a rhyme that delivers a blow even as it asserts his own lyrical ingenuity: "Hiding behind 8 *Mile* and *The Chronic* / *Get Rich but Dies Rhymin'*, this is high science." Using album titles to stand in for the artists with whom they are associated, Nas charges 50 with hiding behind Eminem and Dr. Dre, while riffing on the title of 50's own album *Get Rich or Die Tryin'*. Through the very force of his art, Nas rebukes 50's criticisms while refreshing his own language with a poetic figure.

Wordplay doesn't always rely upon complex games with meaning. Some of the simplest rhetorical figures of all consist of manipulations of sound itself. "Woop! Woop! That's the sound of da police," KRS-One famously chants on the hook of "Sound of da Police" from 1993's *Return of the Boombap*. The unmistakable sound he makes in place of the police siren is an example of *onomatopoeia*, the trope that works by exchanging the thing itself for a linguistic representation of the sound it makes. It would seem impossible for an oral poetry like rap even to contain a concept like onomatopoeia, given that onomatopoeia is defined by the written word. If the sound remains a sound without the middle ground of the page, then onomatopoeia can't exist. So when we speak about onomatopoeia in rap, we are assuming that the lyrics exist in a book of rhymes or at least in a listener's transcription.

Eminem offers a dramatic onomatopoeic example on "Kill You": "invented violence, you vile venomous volatile bitches / vain Vicodin, vrinnn Vrinnn, VRINNN!" That last sound, if you couldn't recognize it, is the sound of a chainsaw (excuse my transcription; I'm sure Em did it better if and when he wrote it down). By combining onomatopoeia with alliteration, he shows the natural progression of one figure to the next. The alliteration in the *v* sounds leads Eminem to surrender to the sound itself through onomatopoeia, which in turn somehow leads him back to a thing once again, the chainsaw. If this all seems rather involved—well, it is. But the brilliance of Eminem's wordplay is that we experience it as effortless lyricism rather than complex poetic negotiation.

Where onomatopoeia celebrates sound itself, two other devices use sonic similarities to play games with meaning. *Homonyms* are two words with the same sound, same spelling, but different meanings—like *fire* (as in "flame") and *fire* (as in "terminate from employment"). *Homophones* are two words with the same sound, different spellings, and different meanings—like *led* and *lead*. Chuck D rhymed on "Bring the Noise" that "they got me in a cell 'cause my records, they sell." "Cell" and "sell" are homophones.

MCs have taken advantage of these types of words to fashion clever wordplay, and in turn transform meaning in the process. For example, Jay-Z's opening verse to Beyoncé's 2006 single "Déjà Vu" goes like this: "I used to run base like Juan Pierre / now I run the bass, high hat, and the snare." Here we have a simile comparing how Jay-Z used to run drugs to how Juan Pierre, the fleet-footed centerfielder for the Dodgers, runs the base pads. This relies upon "base" as a homonym. Rather than stopping there, he follows it up with the next line that flips the homonym into a homophone by introducing "bass" as a drum. An even more ingenious example comes from "Blue Magic," the first single off of Jay-Z's 2007 *American Gangster* album:

> Blame Reagan for making me into a monster
> Blame Oliver North and **IRAN-CONTRA**
> **I RAN CONTRA**band that they sponsored
> Before this rhyming stuff we was in concert.

It testifies to Jay-Z's lyrical ingenuity that even though we fully experience these poetic lines by ear rather than by eye, looking at them on the page calls attention to their individual effects, not just their cumulative impact. Equally as impressive as the homonym is that he delivers it while making a fairly complicated point, all while rhyming four lines together. Lil Wayne achieves a similar effect on his ubiquitous 2008 hit "Lollipop (Remix)" when he rhymes these lines:

Safe sex is great sex, better wear a *LATEX*
'Cause you don't want that *LATE TEXT*
That "I think I'm *LATE" TEXT*

While these are not perfect homophones, they become so through Lil Wayne's performance of the lines. These are a virtuoso's lines, ones that Weezy himself seems to appreciate as he chuckles after delivering them. However, in both Jay-Z and Lil Wayne's rhymes, as complex as the wordplay becomes, the lyrical effect remains one of absolute effortlessness.

Some MCs have taken this same technique and made it not just the basis of a hot line, but the foundation of an entire rhyme style. Rarely is it that a single rhetorical form can essentially define the poetics of not just one MC but of an entire clique. Such is the case with the Diplomats and the figurative trope of antanaclasis. Antanaclasis is when a single word is repeated multiple times, but each time with a different meaning. For the Diplomats, the popularity of it likely began with Cam'ron, the leading member of Dipset, who started his career rapping alongside Mase. Consider the following lines off one of his mix-tape releases: "I flip China White, / my dishes white china / from China." Playing with just two words, he renders them in several distinct permutations. *China White* is a particular variety of heroin. *White china* is a generic term for dishware, and he then goes on to specify that his dishware actually is from China. What might sound like nonsense or repetition for the sake of sound alone soon reveals itself as a rhetorical figure in action.

Of course, this kind of singular focus on a particular trope can sometimes go too far. One of Dipset's youngest members, JR Writer, who calls himself the "Writer of Writers," is considered by some to be one of New York's up-and-coming lyricists. He is well known among rap fans for his numerous mix-tape appearances, especially his Writer's Block series. Like the rest of Dipset, his rhyme style is characterized by his reliance on antanaclasis and other tropes of repetition. Rhymes like the following show him taking his wordplay to just this side of incomprehensibility: "I flip the flip for the flip / Call me a flip-flipper / Then flip-flop in my flip-flops / With strip-strippers." It's hard to imagine antanaclasis going any farther than that. Is this virtuosity or excess? As Prince once said while singing about something else entirely, there's joy in repetition. However, repetition can be overdone, going from pleasing to grating on the ear. The challenge for MCs who craft patterns of repetition in their rhymes is to find a balance between pleasure and monotony.

Unlike some of the other rhetorical schemes in this chapter, alliteration and its cousin, assonance, rely upon oral expression to generate their full effect. Reading a succession of repeated consonants or vowels on the page is nothing like hearing them recited aloud. At least in this regard, then, rap shares something with nursery rhymes: It entertains us by satisfying our ears even before it reaches our mind. Run-DMC knew this when Run began a verse by recalling a famous nursery rhyme chant: "Now Peter Piper picked peppers but Run rock rhymes." In this line alone, Run shows just how (through *alliteration*, in this case) rap reinvents patterned repetition for the hip-hop generation, claiming it as a valid technique for rap lyricism.

As a scheme for repetitive patterning, however, alliteration is only the most obvious technique. *Assonance*, a rhetorical scheme based upon the repetition of vowel sounds, is often upstaged on the page, even when it's clear to the ear. As demonstrated in the previous chapter, it is intimately related to rhyme. But what if the repetition involved is not about sound but about structure?

Anaphora and *epistrophe* are distinct but related rhetorical schemes, both establishing patterns of repeated words. Anaphora is word repetition at the beginning of successive lines, while epistrophe is repetition at the end. If you've ever read Homer's *Iliad* or *Odyssey* or the Bible, then you've seen these forms in action. Both of these schemes serve a particular purpose in oral expression. On a practical level, they facilitate memorization. On a stylistic one, they convey a sense of balance and order. When used in rap, they do both at once. Consider this example of anaphora from the underground Oakland, California, duo Zion I:

> How many times have you watched the sun rise?
> How many times have you looked deep into your lover's eyes?
> How many times have we spit phat rhymes?
> How many times?
> How many times?

The entire song is structured on the repetition of that opening phrase. A series of rhetorical questions illustrating the need for physical and spiritual awakening gains prophetic intensity with each repeated phrase.

Epistrophe is a trickier scheme for rap because rappers usually insist upon ending lines with different—though often rhyming—words. Of course, there are ways out of this constraint. One way is to combine epistrophe with the figurative trope antanaclasis (the use of the same word in different senses). MCs who do this usually get a pass because, though they have failed to rhyme, they have nonetheless done something poetically interesting with the verse.

Some MCs, however, have used epistrophe to great effect, creating incantatory and strongly rhythmic sounds. Ab Liva, for instance, delivers a verse on "Stay from Around Me" of the Clipse's *We Got the Remix* mix-tape on which almost every line ends with "wit it": "Yeah, I get bitter wit it / Make a wrong sign, hitter wit it / I get acquitted wit it / Waistline perfect gotta fit her wit it / I send your soul to the Lord when I fiddle wit it / Yeah, I riddle wit it." And so on. The effect is quite powerful, creating meaning of its own in the repetition of the sound alone.

More controversial are those rappers who make seemingly random repetition an element of their style—often without the benefit of employing words with dual meanings. Repeating the same word without an identifiable pattern is called *repititio*—a kind of lyrical chaos theory for repetition schemes. What it lacks in balance it often makes up for in sound patterning. Juelz Santana, from the aforementioned Dipset, is well known for crafting his wordplay on this principle. These lines from "S.A.N.T.A.N.A." offer an excellent illustration:

> **OKAY**, I'm reloaded. **OKAY**, the heat's loaded.
> **OKAY**, now we rolling, **OKAY**. (Yeah.)
> My .44 piece *TALKING*, sound oh-so-sweet *TALKING*
> Do more, more street *TALKING* than Stone Cold Steve Austin.
> And I bang it *WELL*, slang it *WELL*, shave it *WELL*.
> Hell, you lookin' at a preview of *The Matrix 12*.

Santana's opening six bars contain three sets of repeated words. You may notice one rather surprising thing: with the exception of the half rhyme in the final two lines ("well" with "twelve"), none of these lines rhyme. Instead, he has substituted repetition as a way of giving the verse order. It satisfies the listener's ear by generating some sense of sonic repetition, but without the actual presence of rhyme.

Finally, *epanados* works on the principle of repeating pairs of words in opposite order. When the witches who begin Shakespeare's *Macbeth* utter the line "Fair is foul, and foul is fair" they are using epanados. In rap, it might look like the following verse from a 1980s DMC freestyle: "I'm DMC in the place to be / and the place to be is with DMC." Of course, unlike repititio, which comes across as unrehearsed— even accidental—epanados can often seem overly practiced and forced. As rap continues to evolve in the direction of free forms rather than highly structured ones, it's likely that epanados and other forms like it may go the way of Adidas with the fat laces.

Whether forcing us to think about familiar subjects from startling new perspectives, or nudging us to listen more attentively to the meanings of their intricate constructions, rappers use wordplay to jar us out of our assumptions. It means changing not only what we see, but *how* we see. There is more at stake in rap wordplay than a dope verse or a clever turn of phrase; rather, it just might redefine what we understand as real. Rap at its best insists upon changing the world, or at least changing how the world appears to us, by remaking it in rap's own image. That is precisely why we keep coming back to it. It has the potential to startle us out of our imaginative lethargy to experience life again, as if for the first time. For those who don't take the time or lack the ear to apprehend its lyrical substance, rap will undoubtedly seem like something else entirely—crass, repetitive, and unimaginative. But for those who care to look, rap rewards the effort with the beats and rhymes of new life.

Part Two

Part Two

FOUR

Style

LEGEND HOLDS THAT during a freestyle battle in the late 1980s an unsuspecting rap neophyte broke his own jaw trying to mimic the signature style of "the god MC," Rakim. While it may be apocryphal, the legend testifies to an essential truth about rap: Style reigns supreme.

MCs often talk about style like it is a possession, a lyrical fingerprint distinguishing one MC from all others, even a gift bestowed upon them by a higher power. "God gave me style, God gave me grace / God put a smile on my face," 50 Cent once rhymed. At the same time, rappers also talk about style as something to be switched up, changed up, flipped, and otherwise transformed in the name of lyrical ingenuity. That style can be both identity and diversity at the same time attests to the breadth of meaning the term carries in hip-hop circles. For MCs, style is what you do, but it is also what the people around you do, where and when you happen to live.

To put it another way, while style is a matter of the qualities of an individual artist, it is also the term we use to describe larger definitions: the sound shared by an entire crew, for instance, or the familiar forms of a region, a time period, or a genre. Style has to do both with the artist's conscious crafting of particular attributes into a sonic whole as well as with the audience's reception—often their varying receptions—of those attributes in the music. Q-Tip once rhymed, explaining his popularity, that "ladies love the voice, brothers dig the lyrics." He knew that his style was not just what he made of it, but what *others* made of it as well.

Style describes both what an artist puts into a work of art and what an audience gets out of it. It takes on different meanings when seen from within and from without the process of artistic creation. From within, style involves the way an artist produces a work of art, the sum of the choices that result in the formation of an artistic whole. From without, style involves the way an audience interprets the arrangement of language in a work of art. It defines the terms of individual artists' styles, as well as the habits of larger stylistic groups of which that individual may belong.

The fact that styles are identifiable means that they are at least in part predictable. It is this predictability that allows us to talk meaningfully about "Jay-Z's style" or the "hyphy sound" or the stylistic differences between Miami rap and Atlanta rap, Brooklyn style and Queens style. "We develop schemas for particular musical genres and styles;" writes the recording engineer turned neuroscientist, Daniel J. Levitin, "*style* is just another word for 'repetition.'" What he means by this for our purposes is that styles—whether they belong to individuals or to groups, regions, or genres—take shape only when at least some element of them becomes predictable, when we can conceive schemas or patterns of expectation. Even if it is the predictability of the unpredictable, like in the rhymes of the late Ol' Dirty Bastard, style defines itself through continuity. When we say that some new artist is trying to sound like Lil Wayne, or when we say that Lil Wayne doesn't sound the same way he used to sound, we are working from a stylistic knowledge base that develops even without our conscious awareness of it.

This same principle of style as repetition holds true for rap as a whole. What must it have been like, then, to have been the first person to hear rap music? What must it have been like to have turned on the radio in 1979 and heard a fifteen-minute song with a familiar disco hook, a driving beat, and a group of male voices that weren't quite speaking, weren't quite singing? The majority of rap's audience today never experienced such an epiphany. Most of us have known rap all our lives—maybe even longer.

Researchers have found that we begin to develop our musical knowledge even before we leave the womb, and by age five or six we already have a sophisticated sense of the various musical schemas that correspond to our culture. For those of us exposed to hip hop at an early age—for some of us this means even before birth—rap carries with it an unmistakable familiarity. Its stylistic conventions are apparent; quite literally, our brain is encoded on the neural level with a set of expectations for rap as a genre. We might know, for instance, that rap almost always follows a 4/4 measure with a strong kick-drum downbeat on the one and three and a snare backbeat on the two and four. We might know that this beat is the centerpiece of a rhythmic performance that also includes the MC's voice flowing on top of the track, usually in the pocket of the beat. We might know that these dual rhythms usually predominate over any harmonies and melodies in the song. This is our equipment for listening, things we need never consciously consult that nonetheless define the contours of our relationship to the music.

For those with little or no exposure to rap, this equipment is underdeveloped or missing entirely. Of course, it is possible to learn to love rap, or any other music for which one lacks exposure, but it requires many hours of listening and conscious mental effort. By isolating the elements of style, we reinforce the very neural pathways that allow us to experience rap as pleasurable. Think of this chapter, then, as a road-construction project for your musical mind, helping you build from dirt paths to paved roads and from paved roads to expressways of musical perception.

For the MC, just as for any artist, style is the sum of rules and creativity. Inherent in this definition is the concept of genius, the capacity of particular artists to create new possibilities within the context of inherited forms. Style can describe the characteristic qualities of an individual MC, the dominant mode of a particular time period, as well as the shared aesthetic of a group or even an entire region. It is an umbrella term for a host of different things that MCs have made out of rap's poetic form. As Adam Krims observes, style encompasses "history, geography, and genre all at once, not to mention the constant personal and commercial quest for uniqueness."

When it comes to their styles, rappers are obsessed with novelty, ownership, and freedom. The Beastie Boys crowing "It's the new style!" in 1986 was a declaration of their lyrical independence—ironically, at a time when Run-DMC was writing some of their lyrics. It is one of rap's most common tropes: My style is different from yours. My style is better than yours. Another common boast is claiming innumerable styles. "I got 6 million ways to rhyme: choose one," Common boasts on his second album, *Resurrection*. He also flips this clever bit of wordplay, illustrating the very stylistic freedom he claims: "My style is too developed to be arrested / It's the free style, so now it's out on parole."

Conceiving of style as the product of inherited rules and individual invention connects rap with jazz and the blues, those other dominant forms of African-American musical expression that rely upon both formula and improvisation. All are products of the vernacular process, the artistic impulse to combine the invented and the borrowed, the created and the close at hand. The word *vernacular* comes from the Greek *verna*, which the *Oxford English Dictionary* defines as "a slave born of his master's house." This is no mere etymological footnote; it has profound implications for African-American expressive culture, the only artistic tradition born in slavery. Rap, as the most recent manifestation of the vernacular process in action, extends a tradition of outlaw expression that reaches back to the dawn of the black experience in North America and beyond.

The vernacular, as Ralph Ellison defines it, is "a dynamic *process* in which the most refined styles from the past are continually merged with the play-it-by-eye-and-by-ear improvisations which we invent in our efforts to control our

environment and entertain ourselves." In Ellison's description "the most refined styles" and the "play-it-by-eye-and-
by-ear improvisations" are of equal importance. For an art
form like rap that emerged from the socio-political underground as the voice of young black and brown Americans,
the cultural energy of the vernacular has proved nothing
short of revolutionary.

Rap's most profound achievement is this: it has made
something—and something beautiful—out of almost nothing at all. Two turntables, a microphone, and a lyrical style
define rap as the epitome of African-American vernacular
culture. "Hip-hop is a beautiful culture," Mos Def told the
Los Angeles Times in 2004. "It's inspirational, because it's a
culture of survivors. You can create beauty out of nothingness." Rap may be the music of the street corner rather than
the conservatory, but mastering its verbal art requires as
much attention to craft as the most rarefied forms of artistic
expression. So while rap's spirit is unquestionably revolutionary, its form is traditional. Rap style is always balanced somewhere along this axis.

To say that rap often emerges out of nothingness, however, is not to say that it comes from nowhere. MCs tend to
make a big deal about their place of birth. Anyone who's
ever been to a Mos Def concert has undoubtedly heard him
shout "Where Brooklyn at?" And if you're at a Roots show,
Black Thought will tell you, more than once, that he's repre-
sentin' Philly. While rock musicians often open concerts by
telling you where *you're* from ("Hello, Chattanooga!"), rappers usually start by telling you where *they're* from. This is
more than a matter of geography, it's an article of faith and
an element of style.

It makes sense that hip hop would be obsessed with place. Representing for your borough, or even your block, has long been a motivating interest in rap. "I wanted to put Queens on the map," a young LL Cool J announced. Such insistence on geography no doubt in part originated out of deep-seated rivalries across and among New York's boroughs. It also drew from a deeper, more sustaining source: the desire to have pride in one's community, even if—especially if— that community was denigrated by outsiders. Rappers created a self-fulfilling prophecy: by taking pride in where they were from, they gave where they're from a reason to be proud.

At the same time, hip hop fostered from its beginning a universalist aesthetic as well. As the product of a mixed-cultural heritage, drawing from African-American, Afro-Caribbean, Latin, and even white punk-rock roots, hip hop was both a democratic and democratizing force; in other words, it made a place for the very equality it manifested in its amalgamated art. On the 1987 hip-hop classic "I Ain't No Joke" Rakim gave voice to this inclusive sensibility:

> Now if you're from uptown, Brooklyn-bound,
> The Bronx, Queens, or Long Island Sound,
> Even other states come right and exact,
> It ain't where you're from, it's where you're at.

The inclusion that hip hop offered, as Rakim suggests, did not come free; it demanded fealty to form, a knowledge and appreciation of the culture, and a certain level of mastery. Rakim, from Long Island himself, was voicing an appeal to collective consciousness or, as George Clinton once proclaimed, to one nation under a groove. With hip hop we could all get down, and *be* down if we would only "come right and exact."

Eight years later, Mobb Deep would turn Rakim's credo on its head, reasserting the primacy of territory. Spitting his verse on "Right Back at You," Havoc rhymes, "Fuck where you're at, kid, it's where you're from / 'Cause where I'm from, niggas pack nuthin' but the big guns." For Havoc, hip hop had everything to do with place. "Queensbridge, that's where I'm from," he rhymes, "The place where stars are born and phony rappers get done / Six blocks and you might not make it through / What you gonna do when my whole crew is blazing at you?" Behind the venomous threats is an assertion of pride, in place, but also in style. "Queens rappers have a special style," the West Coast veteran Ice-T admits. It's hard to dispute his analysis. The six blocks of Queensbridge housing projects alone have produced dozens of rap standouts including Marley Marl, MC Shan, Roxanne Shanté, MC Butchy B, Craig G, Nas, Big Noyd, and Cormega. While they differ in talent and temperament, they undoubtedly share a certain spirit. If Queensbridge has a sound, it embodies certain qualities: dark, grimy production with rhymes to match, vividly rendered pictures of urban realities.

If a style can be as specific as a six-block radius, then it only stands to reason that it can encompass an entire region. In hip hop's first decade, when New York dominated, it made sense that the stylistic differences would be on the micro level—borough to borough, even block to block. But as rap started to gain ground in the West Coast, the East Coast sound started to coalesce.

At the height of tensions in the mid-1990s, the difference between East and West Coast rap culture was so great that Dr. Dre could reasonably be shocked to discover that his album *The Chronic*, now recognized as one of the two or three most influential hip-hop recordings of all time, was being played just as much in New York as in L.A. Do these traditional stylistic divisions of region still matter now that hip hop has grown into a global phenomenon? Has the context for them shifted now that we can conceivably compare the rap styles of Brazil or South Africa with the United States as a whole, rather than East or West, Midwest or South? Broadly considered, rap's center of gravity has moved from East (specifically New York) to West (specifically L.A.) to South (specifically Atlanta) over the years. This is not to say great music hasn't come from other places, from Cleveland, for example, or from Karachi, but that rap often takes on the character of a particular locality. Perhaps it's a matter of where you're from *and* where you're at. Regardless, it is ultimately the responsibility of individual artists to define personal styles out of a combination of their individual genius and the influences that surround them.

As important as geography is to rap, we come to know the music through the range and versatility of individual artists. When it comes to experiencing any art form, it's almost always like this: We long for the specific rather than the general. If we wish to read a poem, we want one by Robert Frost or Elizabeth Bishop or Pablo Neruda, not the idea of a poem in the abstract. When we go to an art museum, we're drawn to particular periods—the impressionists, the abstract expressionists—or even particular painters, Monet, Kandinsky. The same holds true for rap. We want to hear Tupac's prophetic baritone, or Biggie's graveyard humor; we want Jay-Z's understated complexity, Common's smoothed-out delivery, or Talib Kweli's dense lyricism. Certain MCs have a distinctive personal style, some quality of voice, of theme, of rhythm, or any combination of these that forges a distinguishable character to their lyricism. What is it that separates one from another, that makes one better than another? What is it that keeps us coming back to hear them time and time again?

On the inner sleeve of his second solo album, 1987's *How Ya Like Me Now*, Kool Moe Dee attempted to answer these questions for rap with the first-ever Rap Report Card. He evaluates twenty-four of his rap contemporaries on a ten-point scale in ten different categories, such as "vocabulary," "articulation," "creativity," "voice," "sticking to themes," and "innovating rhythms." Never one for humility, he awards himself an A+, a grade he shares with two other star students, hip-hop pioneers Melle Mel and Grandmaster Caz. But while his report card is marred by poetic injustices (Public Enemy rates only a B; the Beastie Boys, a C) and inaccuracies (he misspells the names of Rakim and Biz Markie, among others), it nonetheless represents something remarkable in rap's history. Kool Moe Dee makes explicit something that rap fans often think about but rarely articulate: that an MC's style consists of identifiable elements of form, and that we can judge an MC's greatness using these elements.

The report card, while enlightening and entertaining, tells only part of the story. An MC's greatness is never simply the sum of particular formal accomplishments; listeners experience rap in the totality of its performance, as the sum of its styles. Studying style requires that we key into the most essential elements that define that particular MC's expression. Consider, for instance, the long-standing argument among hip-hop heads over whether Tupac or the Notorious B.I.G. was the better MC. Among the many debates rap fans have over style—underground or mainstream, Dirty South or East Coast, Kanye or 50 Cent—the Pac and Big debate is among the most passionate, particularly in the years since their violent, unresolved, and untimely deaths. When MTV gathered a panel of hip-hop experts to compile, with the help of an online fan poll, a list of the greatest MCs of all time, both artists made the list: Biggie coming in third and Tupac coming in second (with Jay-Z in first). But the proximity of their ranking belies the more divided opinion held by many listeners. Few people who love Biggie's style have the same love for Pac's, and vice versa. They may respect the other MC, but when it comes to deciding what they want to hear, the difference is usually clear.

I once helped a good friend, a former editor at *The Source*, drive a U-Haul truck from Miami to Boston. Along the way we had a lot of debates on rap, as was our custom, but none proved more heated than our Biggie/Tupac debate. He was in the Tupac camp; Biggie, he said, wouldn't even make his top fifty MCs. Pac had that voice, that passionate delivery; he also had a more impressive diversity of themes. I was a Biggie guy, if somewhat more moderate; while I put Biggie in my top five, Pac at least made the top fifteen. Biggie had the superior flow, sharper storytelling abilities, more clever wordplay, and the greater sense of humor. I could admire Tupac's rhymes, but I could love Biggie's. And so as we made our way up Interstate 95, we commenced a series of fruitless attempts to convince each other by cranking out track-for-track comparisons from the tinny speakers of the moving truck. As the songs played, we'd punctuate them with our own recitation of the lyrics or glosses on the meaning and eloquence of particular lines.

I think it was somewhere in the middle of "Hail Mary" from Tupac's Makaveli album, *The Don Killuminati: The 7 Day Theory*, when it dawned on me that, as fun as this game was, we might just be missing the point. Our preference for one MC's style over the other's says at least as much about what we value as listeners as it does about the inherent accomplishment of the particular artist. My friend and I were both listening in our own terms, with our own largely unacknowledged and unexamined aesthetic values at work. This is, after all, what listeners do; this is what we call personal taste.

But understanding style requires something different. Style asks us also to listen in the terms the artists themselves establish, to judge them in the ways their art asks to be judged. To point out the absence of Tupac's passionate introspection in Biggie's lyrics or the dearth of Biggie's punning wordplay in Pac's is to demand of those artists something neither ever intended to provide. If we listen to them on their own stylistic terms, however, we can judge them against the forms of excellence to which they aspire.

"Technically, Tupac wasn't a great rapper," writes *Rolling Stone* music critic Anthony DeCurtis, "but he invented a compelling, brooding self in song and image that made his failings completely irrelevant. . . . The man became the music—and the words." DeCurtis is heading in the right direction, but I would take his claim even further. Tupac *was* a great rapper, provided we judge his technique against the ideal it posits for itself rather than our own abstractions of taste. While there is an important place for discerning, as Kool Moe Dee once did, the constitutive elements of style that we can use to judge the value of individual MCs, there is also a vital need to work from the opposite direction: to begin with individual styles—Biggie's, Pac's, whomever's—and move inductively toward an understanding of an individual style and the combination of traits upon which that style is based. And so we give extra weight to wordplay when considering Biggie's style because his lyrics call so much attention to his arrangement of language, his imagery, and puns. When evaluating Tupac, however, wordplay plays a lesser role because it is something he seems consciously to downplay in his lyrics, perhaps not wanting to detract from the power of his direct expression—that connection between man and music that DeCurtis celebrates.

Addressing the Biggie versus Tupac comparison, Shock-G of Digital Underground suggests that their value lies as much in the way we, the listeners, hear them as it does in their own stylistic achievements.

> Biggie's gonna win hands down when you're talking about flow. Strictly from a rhythm standpoint, Biggie is the swinger. He swings like a horn-player over jazz. . . . When people say 'Pac is the best rapper of all time, they don't just mean he's the best rapper, they just mean what he had to say was most potent, most relevant.

While Biggie could deliver a dope line just by spelling his name ("B-I-G-P-O-P-P-A / No info for the DEA"), Tupac's lyrical strength came from the passion of his performance, like a streetwise preacher working the pulpit. It is our great fortune as listeners, of course, that we don't have to choose between the two MCs, the two styles. Understanding style requires us to hold two things in our minds at once: a sense of the full range of potential parts in lyrical expression, and the particular combination of those parts that goes into making the style of any one MC.

Rap style consists of many elements, perhaps the most significant of which are *voice*, the unique timbre of an MC's expression and the tonal range of that expression; *technique*, the formal elements (the most significant of which is flow) that distinguish one MC's performance from another's; and *content*, the subject matter of an MC's lyrics. These three elements alone can go a long way toward explaining things we know intuitively: like why Biggie is so different from Tupac, why certain artists go pop and others remain in the underground, why old-school differs from new-school or East differs from West, which differs from Midwest, which differs from South.

Some stylistic elements, of course, are easier to adopt than others. Voice may be the most difficult to replicate if only because not everyone who wants to sound like Biggie can sound like Biggie. Yet enough have tried—Shyne and Guerilla Black come to mind—that it seems that even this element of style is not beyond imitation. (For living proof, check out the YouTube clip where comedian Aries Spears freestyles live on radio while impersonating the voices of LL Cool J, Snoop Dogg, DMX, and Jay-Z. It's nothing short of amazing.) Certain MCs have staked their careers on the unique appeal of their voices, the physical instruments of their art. 50 Cent was an underground MC until a bullet lodged in his jaw transformed his vocal timbre, endowing him with his unmistakable, slightly sinister slur. DMX has patterned his style on the same guttural barks and growls of his numerous canine pets. And for all Tupac's stylistic great-

ness, the thing we remember most is the voice—the rich, res-
onant baritone that dipped and dived with the phrasings of a
country preacher or a city pimp. "A distinct voice tone is the
identity and signature of the Rapper, and it adds flavor to
anything being said," KRS-One explains. "Rappers with no
distinct voice tone are soon forgotten, whereas Rappers
with distinct and unique voice tones are always remembered
and identified by their audience." Rap is also the music of the
human voice; it is tone and timbre, combing with rhythm
and, increasingly, harmony and melody, to make song.

Technique is the element of style most open to imitation. Truly groundbreaking MCs are those who develop individual styles that can be adopted and adapted by other
artists—or even an entire generation of artists. Melle Mel's
emphasizing words on the two and four, Rakim's multisyllabic rhymes, Big Daddy Kane's fast and slow flow, all of
these innovations of technique made impacts that extended
well beyond the originator's own personal style. It is difficult
to claim ownership over a technique. Unlike the sound of
one's voice, a way of saying something is easily disassociated
from its originator; indeed, it almost demands to be disassociated. Rap was born out of the vernacular process of creative
individuals borrowing from existing sources and adding
something distinctly their own. So the question for those
MCs who borrow Rakim's rhymes or Kane's flow is, what did
you add of your own?

Rap's critics often claim that rap lacks thematic range,
that few rappers are adding anything of their own. All MCs
ever talk about is how many women they have, how much
money they stack, what cars they drive, and how much better they are at everything they do than anyone else around.

Those of us who listen to rap know that this just isn't true. Rap has a broad expressive range, but who can blame those who are exposed only to hip hop's commercial hits from drawing such limited conclusions?

Sense follows sound in rap. Rap lyrics only rarely introduce new ideas. But rap is not alone in this. "I suspect that the freshest and most engaging poems most often don't come from *ideas* at all," observes the poet Ted Kooser of literary verse. "Ideas are orderly, rational, and to some degree logical. They come clothed in complete sentences, like 'Overpopulation is the cause of all the problems in the world.' Instead, poems are trigged by catchy twists of language or little glimpses of life." When Kooser mentions "catchy twists of language" and "little glimpses of life" he might as well be speaking directly about rap. Rap achieves both of these, whether it comes clothed in Immortal Technique's scathing political critique of George W. Bush on "Bin Laden" or Yung Joc's playful, amoral celebration of the crack trade on "Coffee Shop." Poetry, in other words, is value neutral, though listeners certainly are not. Rap asks that each rhyme be judged on its own terms, the terms by which it presents itself. Rap asks to be judged not simply as pure content, but as content expressed in specific, poetic language. They are inseparable. As Terry Eagleton notes, "the language of a poem is *constitutive* of its ideas."

What happens, though, when a rap artist sets out to transform the ideas that go into the music? What does this require of the poetic craft? The career of Kanye West offers a compelling case study in what happens when an artist sets out to change the game.

Kanye burst on the scene as a rapper in 2004. By that time, he had already produced chart-topping hits, like the distinctive soul-sampled Jay-Z smashes "This Can't Be Life" and "Izzo (H.O.V.A.)." Critics were quick to praise Kanye's debut album, *The College Dropout*, for what many saw as his fresh sound and original subject matter. Here was a rapper not just rhyming about girls, cars, and clothes (although he certainly did that as well), but about organized religion, the excesses of consumerism, even folding shirts at the Gap. In an interview with the website universalurban.com just before the release of *The College Dropout*, Kanye reflected upon the formation of his distinctive style. His explanation speaks not only to his own process of creation but to the common challenge of all artists trying to break new stylistic ground in a medium dominated by a handful of trendsetters.

> It's like if you wanna rap like Jay[-Z], it's hard to rap like Jay and not rap about what Jay is rapping about. So what I did is incorporate all these different forms of rap together—like I'll use old school [rhythm] patterns, I come up with new patterns in my head every day. Once I found out exactly how to rap about drugs and exactly how to rap about "say no to drugs," I knew that I could fill the exact medium between that. My persona is that I'm the regular person. Just think about whatever you've been through in the past week, and I have a song about that on my album.

Kanye's comments underscore several essential truths about style in rap. Contrary to many people's assumptions, in rap content often follows style. In other words, the stylistic models an aspiring MC imitates often dictate the content of the rhymes as well. It would be hard to imagine an MC, for instance, with 50 Cent's style and Lauryn Hill's content. There is something essential in 50 Cent's style—the constitutive elements of his poetics—that lends itself to a particular set of themes: in his case, women, cars, his thug past, and exaltation of his own lyrical greatness.

Another significant lesson to draw from Kanye's remarks is that style is often the product of the self-conscious construction of a lyrical identity, or persona. For Kanye, that persona would be the common man—a garden-variety identity in most literary traditions, but a surprisingly underdeveloped one in a hip-hop tradition that trades upon the projection of self-aggrandizing and larger-than-life images. Of course the irony of these comments is apparent in light of Kanye's notoriously outsized ego, and yet he does project a common *persona* at times in his rhymes, even if he as a *person* is far from it. Throughout *The College Dropout* and intermittently on his subsequent releases, Kanye extends a rap tradition of self-deprecation that, while far overshadowed by its opposite, still holds an essential place in rap's history. As he rhymes on "All Falls Down," perhaps his finest lyrical performance on the album, "We all self-conscious, I'm just the first to admit it." This theme of vulnerability reflects itself in a style that is sometimes halting and awkward, vocal tones that he comically exaggerates, and unorthodox rhythms and rhymes that call our attention to what's new in his lyrics. Whatever else Kanye West's career reveals, it shows that a revolution in rap's themes must begin with a revolution in rap's poetics. All artists must face up to Kanye's dilemma at some point in their development: how to craft an individual voice out of the myriad influences available. This is the definition of personal style.

I once taught a student who said he liked to rhyme. He knew that I was writing this book, so he offered me a CD with several of his songs. I played it on my drive home. What I heard, though it surprised me at the time, shouldn't have been at all unexpected: I heard 50 Cent—well, not exactly 50 Cent, but my student's very best impersonation of 50's signature flow and familiar gun talk. His alias probably should have tipped me off; I won't reveal it here, but it was something very nearly like "Half a Dollar" or "48 Cent." In ways both conscious and not, my student had patterned his style so closely upon 50's that even his ad libs seemed straight off of "Candy Shop" or "I Get Money." He actually wasn't doing a bad job of it, either; the production value of his homemade tracks was respectable; and his flow, though not exactly his own, embodied that same sense of offhanded swagger that is 50's greatest strength as a rapper.

Part of me, however, couldn't help but think it was a little absurd for this college sophomore, a good student attending a predominantly white suburban liberal-arts college in sunny Southern California, to be spitting bars more at home in a hardscrabble neighborhood of South Queens. Then again, I suppose it's no more absurd than 50 spitting these same lines today from the tony Connecticut compound where he currently resides. Driving back to campus the next morning, I played the tracks again. This time, instead of just hearing the imitation, I heard something else: the birth of a young artist's style.

Style often starts as a form of jealousy. Someone does something that you want to do, but don't know how to do and it motivates you to figure it out. You begin to build this body of influences until you have a particular blend that is distinctly your own. Style is amalgamation.

No style is completely original. Certainly there's a sliding scale of originality that stretches from the completely copied to the wholly original. Most artists reside in between, shifting along the axis at different points in their careers—even at different points in particular rhymes. This is most evident with young artists still searching for their voices. A necessary part of the process of development includes imitation. Out of that imitation, innovation is often born. It only makes sense that aspiring MCs will want to model their style upon the most successful artists of the moment. My student's choosing 50 Cent made intuitive sense, given that 50 is one of the best-selling rap artists of all time. Certainly this choice came at a cost to the variety of my student's themes and the authenticity of his voice, but it made sense from a poetic standpoint. Keats began by modeling himself after Shakespeare. Hughes modeled himself after Carl Sandburg and Walt Whitman. This is what we mean by *tradition*.

50 Cent himself had to learn how to rhyme from someone, too. Despite his claims, it seems it wasn't God that gave him style, but a humbler source, the late Jam Master Jay of the legendary Run-DMC. In his memoir, *From Pieces to Weight*, 50 relates the story of his MC education, a revealing record of style in the making.

> I didn't know what I was doing. I had never written a rhyme. But I looked at it like it was my chance to get out of the drug game, so I hopped on it. I wrote to the CD [Jam Master Jay had given him], rapping from the time the beat started to the time the beat ended. I went back to Jay's studio a few days later and played him what I had done. When he heard it, he started laughing. He

liked the rhyme, but he said that he had to teach me song format—how to count bars, build verses, everything. On the CD I had given him, I was just rambling, talking about all kinds of shit. There was no structure, no concept, nothing. But the talent was there.

Talent is critical, but alone it falls short of producing art. Style begins with the basics, with the formal rules of the genre as much as with inspiration or excellence. 50's story is a rather common coming-of-age tale for rap. Snoop Dogg recalls a similar moment of stylistic realization. "I wasn't a good writer, but in a battle I could beat anybody," he recalls. "But as far as songwriting, I didn't know how to write. Then once I got with Dr. Dre he showed me how to turn my 52 bar raps into 16 bar raps." In both these cases it is curious to note that these lyricists didn't learn rap form from other lyricists but from producers, suggesting an essential link between lyrical and musical forms in rap.

When Eminem released his independent debut album, *Infinite*, in 1996, the few critics who heard it (the original release was a little over a thousand copies—all on vinyl and cassette) accused him of biting the styles of other artists, most notably Nas. Eminem admits as much, and looks back upon the album as a crucial step in his stylistic development. "Obviously, I was young and influenced by other artists," he recalls, "and I got a lot of feedback saying that I sounded like Nas and AZ. *Infinite* was me trying to figure out how I wanted my rap style to be, how I wanted to sound on the mic and present myself. It was a growing stage." Eminem's remarks key into the essential elements of style: the qualities of voice or, as he puts it, "how I wanted to sound on the mic"; and the formation of persona, or how he wanted to "present himself."

Eminem, like 50, Snoop, and my former student, made a conscious effort to define the elements of his personal style. For those critics who consider rap unsophisticated and formless, even for those rap fans who give little thought to how the music is made, it will undoubtedly come as a surprise to learn that MCs most often pursue their craft with such a conscious awareness of form. While many MCs have no formal musical training, they nonetheless have learned the necessary terminology or created a vocabulary of their own to describe the elements of their craft.

Rakim brought formal musical training as a jazz saxophonist to his rhyme style. It certainly informed his phrasing and his rhythmic sensibilities. He also brought a keen awareness of language and its relation to these musical elements. "My style of writing, I love putting a lot of words in the bars, and it's just something I started doing," he explained to the *Village Voice* in 2006. "Now it's stuck with me. I like being read. The way you do that is by having a lot of words, a lot of syllables, different types of words." This is a remarkable statement coming from one of rap's standard bearers: *I like being read*. Rakim is claiming for himself, and by extension for rap as a genre, a fundamental poetic identity, a necessary linguistic style to accompany the musical one.

Another MC who uses his voice as an instrument, developing a style conscious of both the linguistic and the musical identities, is Ludacris. In a revealing interview he makes a case for what makes his rap style distinctive.

> But as far as what makes me unique when it comes to verses and things of that nature, I would definitely say that when it comes to doing sixteen bars, whether I am featured on somebody else's

song or whether I am doing it myself, I am just not afraid to take it to the next level—doing something that I know no other artists would do—even with styling, metaphors or whatever. Because if there is anything . . . I want to be known as the most *versatile* MC out there. Whether it is who raps the best with other artists; or who kicks the best metaphors; or who raps slow, or over any kind of beat—whatever. That's me! I think that is what separates me from the rest.

Rap styles are far from static. Though an MC may become known, like Ludacris, for a signature style, it is still possible to innovate within those terms. Some artists evolve quite dramatically, expanding their stylistic identities in ways broad and deep. Lil Wayne's remarkable emergence as a respected lyricist over the past several years came as a result of dramatic stylistic growth. Similarly, Busta Rhymes has transformed over the years from what was essentially a novelty rapper, good as a guest artist or on a hook, to a multifaceted rhymer capable of carrying an entire album.

A very few artists, however, seem to have emerged on the scene full-grown, like Athena from the head of Zeus. Jay-Z was as good on the first track from his debut, *Reasonable Doubt,* as he has ever been since, which is to say that he was something like a legend from the start. Only Jay-Z himself, perhaps, could look back on his early days in rap and see a stylistic transformation. In a revealing interview with Kelefa Sanneh published in the *New York Times* he offered this self-assessment: "I was speeding," he said. "I was saying a hundred words a minute. There were no catchphrases, there were no hooks within the verses. I was very wordy. . . . I don't know that I've gotten better. I think that I've definitely gotten more rounded."

Rap style, however, is not simply about counting bars or building verses. It's not even about ill metaphors and dope rhymes. It is more than the sum of its forms. In addition to the conscious level of craft, it contains an ineffable quality of art. "I honestly never sat down and said 'OK, here's my style,' because my whole thing was knowing everyone's style," explains Bun B, half of southeast Texas's legendary UGK. "Everything I've ever written has bits and pieces of everything I've ever heard. Any rapper who tells you different is a liar. You can't write a book if you've never read a book. . . . So the more rap I learned, the more I was able to bring to rap when I decided to rap. But this was all subconscious." Rap, explains Bun B, is an amalgamated art. It relies upon the vernacular exercise of the individual artist working through the influences close at hand to create something new. The fact that this often occurs subconsciously is part of the mystery of poetic creation.

Poets and songwriters of all types often speak of a zone they reach during the process of composition, a mental state that approximates that of a trance. William Butler Yeats described it this way, echoing Bun B's words across three-quarters of a century, "Style is almost unconscious. I know what I have tried to do, little what I have done." Yeats suggests a difference between artistic aims ("what I tried to do") and artistic achievement ("what I have done") that mirrors the relation between creation and consumption, the artists and the audience.

The poet Frances Mayes offers a more concrete definition, defining poetic style as consisting of "characteristic words and images, prevalent concerns, tone of voice, pattern of syntax, and form. When we read enough of an author, we begin to know the kind of power he has over language and the resources of language at his disposal. What makes us recognize the author, even if a poem is not identified, is style." Style is therefore something that the artist constructs, though often in an "unconscious" state, that the audience can ultimately identify.

Rappers, like anyone else, are subject to popular taste. When a rapper introduces a truly distinctive style—like Melle Mel or Big Daddy Kane, and more recently, like Eminem or Andre 3000—they are bound to have imitators. And while cynics might suggest that these imitators are simply trying to cash in on the popularity of a new sound, they might simply be trying to master rap's difficult form. Every artist in every genre goes through an early phase of imitation. But where a painter or a jazz pianist will likely be able to hone their crafts and develop their personal styles away from the attention of a mass audience, rappers are more likely to be scooped up and packaged for sale well before they've finished their artistic maturation. This is partly because rap is dominated by men who debut at a young age, from their teens into their twenties, and only rarely after thirty. And, yes, it is also a result of a revenue model in which A&Rs are constantly on the lookout for young talent that fits a certain preestablished (and profitable) artistic profile.

Rap's growing commercialization risks stunting the music's stylistic diversity. "Today we take rhyme styles for granted," hip-hop legend KRS-One said. "On *Criminal Minded* those rhyme styles you hear were original. They hadn't been heard before. The album had originality and we lack so much of that today. It seems that if one rapper comes out with a style, twenty others come after him. Hip hop now, what it has become, is just not what we intended it to be. When *Criminal Minded* came out, Big Daddy Kane had his own style, Rakim still has his own style, Kool G Rap, Biz Markie. We've lost cultural continuity because hip-hop has gone from being a culture to being a product."

The product-oriented approach to hip hop that KRS-One talks about creates a stylistic tension, resulting in a host of rappers who sound alike in an art form that celebrates originality and shuns imitation. Among rap's many paradoxes is this one: It is an art form based upon borrowing, and yet it punishes stealing like no other. Rap is a vernacular art, which is to say it takes its shape from a fusion of individual innovation and preexisting forms. Think of Missy Elliott borrowing the chorus from Frankie Smith's "Double Dutch Bus," but flipping it into a funky hook on "Gossip Folks." Or DJ Premier sampling Chuck D's counting for Notorious B.I.G.'s classic "Ten Crack Commandments."

Rap is nothing if not an amalgamated art, comprising bits and pieces, loose ends reordered and reconceived in ways that both announce their debt and assert their creative independence from their sources. If the case for the musical virtuosity of the DJ hasn't yet been made, then it should. Wynton Marsalis couldn't build a track with as much rhythmic variety and sonic layering as the RZA or Hi-Tek or Just Blaze. These men are musicians, even if their instruments are two turntables, a mixing board, and ProTools. It is the ultimate postmodern musical form. Born of pastiche, rap instrumentals often assemble something new out of the discarded fragments of other songs, shaping order out of chaos.

The same process of repetition and re-creation holds for the MC's lyrics as well. Think of how many MCs have started their rhymes off, à la Rakim, "It's been a long time. . . ." Rap relies on shared knowledge, a common musical and lyrical vocabulary accessible to all. At the same time, few charges are as damning to an MC as being called a biter. Biting, or co-opting another person's style or even specific lines, qualifies as a high crime in hip hop's code of ethics and aesthetics. Rap polices the boundary between borrowing and theft in ways that at times seems arbitrary.

In early 2005 a mix started circulating through hip-hop radio that featured a litany of Jay-Z lines preceded by their source in other MC's lyrics. Depending on where you stood, "I'm Not a Writer, I'm a Biter" was either proof positive that Jigga was bringing nothing original to rap or, to the contrary, further evidence of his greatness—his ability to be original while still referencing some of the classic lines in hip-hop history. Jay drew his inspiration most often from the Notorious B.I.G., sometimes repeating his lyrics word for word, albeit in the new context of his own verse. The fact that Jay-Z, regarded by many as one of the greatest if not the greatest MC of all time, would so often resort to such lyrical allusions (and that he would also be the source of other artists' borrowing) testifies to one of the foundational truths about rap. Rap is an art born, in part, of imitation.

Imitation, however, is not always biting, though the line of demarcation is sometimes blurry. Biting suggests a flagrant disregard for the integrity of another's art, a lazy practice of passing off someone else's creativity as your own. Imitation in an artistic context means charging another's words with your own creativity and, in the process, creating something that is at once neither his nor yours, and yet somehow both. Art through the ages has followed this same creative practice of free exchange. Shakespeare drew many of his plots, including classics like *Hamlet,* from Holinshed's *Chronicles.* T. S. Eliot's *Waste Land* riffs on everything from ragtime lyrics to sacred Sanskrit texts.

What happens, though, when such artistic freedom meets rap's culture of commerce? Rappers and their fans often talk in a language of ownership, as if something as illusory as style can come with a deed. Sometimes this protection is simply a reflex, a habit of being perhaps drawn from what KRS-One called the "reality of lack" that many rappers experienced growing up in poor communities. If you have something that's valuable, hold on to it so that everyone knows that it's yours. Add to that the fact that signature styles, even signature lines, can be the stuff of significant wealth in today's rap marketplace and the stakes of what might otherwise have been an aesthetic tussle become much, much greater.

While one can certainly make a reasonable claim to a limited kind of ownership, the natural state of any art form is freedom. Culture is a commodity, not simply in a capitalistic system, but in *any* human society. Artists learn from other artists. Artists "steal" from other artists—and it is not simply the inferior artists who do so. "If there is something to steal, I steal it!" Pablo Picasso once said. The concept of theft in art is complex. While we should resist any effort to misrepresent the history of culture, we also must resist attempts to restrict its free exchange. The moment an MC records a rap—in fact, the moment that MC spits a verse in front of someone other than his own reflection—is the moment culture liberates itself from context.

Speaking about black American culture as a whole, Ralph Ellison once noted that despite our reasonable desires to protect it from outside influence, the fact of the matter is that all cultural creations become common property in a way when presented to the public. "I wish there could be some control of it," Ellison said in a 1973 interview, "but there cannot be control over it, except in this way: through those of us who write and who create using what is there to use in a most eloquent and transcendent way." The individual artist's eloquence and transcendence confer stylistic originality upon shared cultural sources. "I'm not a separatist," Ellison explains earlier in the interview. "The imagination is integrative. That's how you make the new—by putting something else with what you've got." Here Ellison is defining the vernacular process, the act of "putting something else with what you've got." Rap may be the best contemporary example of this principle in action.

Lil Wayne provides a perfect illustration of how conscious imitation can also achieve lyrical innovation on "Dr. Carter," where he not only repeats another artist's line, but does so in celebration of its excellence and in defiance of the risks of being labeled a biter. "Dr. Carter" is a conceptual song in which Weezy takes on the role of a rap physician, diagnosing and treating various rap illnesses like lack of concepts, failure of originality, and wack flow. He spits the following lines on the second verse:

> Now hey, kid—plural, I graduated
> "'Cause you could get through anything if Magic made it."
> And that was called recycling, r.e., reciting
> Something 'cause you just like it so you say it just like it.
> Some say it's biting but I say it's enlightening.
> Besides, Dr. Kanye West is one of the brightest.

Riffing off Kanye's familiar line from "Can't Tell Me Nothing" ("No, I already graduated / And you can live through anything if Magic made it"), Wayne pays tribute even as he displays his own poetic artistry with rhyme ("recycling," "reciting," "biting," "enlightening") and repetition (of "re" as well as the dual meanings of "just like it"). What separates "biting" and "enlightening" is the difference between mere repetition and repetition with a difference. It comes down to a question of ownership, a fraught concept when it concerns something like art.

An equally compelling circumstance of art and ownership concerns the commerce conducted behind the scenes between writers who don't perform their lyrics and performers who don't write their own. The ghostwriter is perhaps the most shadowy figure in rap, cloaked in controversy and obscured out of necessity to protect the credibility of the performer. Ghostwriting, or one artist supplying lyrics to be delivered by another artist, usually for a fee, has been around since rap's birth. While few rappers will admit to using one, many rappers have boasted about being one. "I'm a ghostwriter, I'm the cat that you don't see / I write hits for rappers you like and charge 'em a fee," Mad Skillz rhymes on "Ghostwriter." Or, "Check the credits, S. Carter, ghostwriter / and for the right price, I can even make yo' shit tighter," Jay-Z spits on "Ride or Die."

As a consequence of this close association between writer and performer, rap has traditionally made little room for something like a cover tune. With the exception of groups like the Roots who sometimes perform other artists' songs during their concerts as tributes and as demonstrations of their musical virtuosity, rap has relatively few instances of

MCs rhyming the lyrics of another song in its entirety. Certainly rap has relied heavily on lyrical samples from past rhymes, or from allusive references to them, but rarely has an entire verse, much less a song, been repeated by another artist. Hip hop, it would seem, has no room for standards. This is true for an entire song, but many artists borrow the structure of a verse, including an entire line or set of lines, from previous songs. And reproduction on the levels of theme, image, and expression is common—even to the point of limiting the expressive range of artists to a handful of tried and true themes.

Yet as long as rap has been around, so has the ghostwriter. Sometimes the transaction between performer and ghostwriter has been behind the scenes, other times out in the open. In the 1980s Big Daddy Kane ghostwrote for a host of popular artists, but only the closest observers seemed to take notice. For Kane, as for any ghostwriter, the primary challenge was one of style. How do you write rhymes that authentically come across as another person's voice? How do you embody another artist's style? In a revealing interview with Brian Coleman, Kane offered these observations about ghostwriting for two different artists, Shanté and Biz Markie:

> Writing for Biz was in a whole different style [from mine], so that could be a challenge. But Fly Ty wanted Shanté to have my style, so I wrote for her in that way, and it wasn't a problem, of course. Biz had invented this whole different style and wanted to flow like that—he just couldn't always work the words out. So I wrote in that style for him. Because it was different, the way I wrote for him, it didn't sound like nothin' that would come from me, so it was harder to tell. Shanté would always tell people that I wrote rhymes for her. It wasn't a big deal. The Biz thing was something

that we kept on the hush. Anybody that was really into the art-work and reading all the credits on albums could put one and one together and figure it out, but it wasn't something we mentioned back then.

Kane makes an important distinction between style and songwriting. Biz, he says, had "invented this whole different style," he just "couldn't always work the words out." Style, in this case, is a quality that at once transcends words and is nonetheless bound up in them. Biz Markie created a persona as the clown prince of hip hop with songs like "Picking Boogers" and "Just a Friend." He used his beatboxing alongside his slow, thick-tongued flow to craft a distinctive vocal style, certainly distinct from the smooth, articulate delivery of Kane. It is a testament to the various strengths of both artists that they both are remembered as distinctive lyrical stylists from their era.

Ghostwriting's long tradition in hip hop is not necessarily at odds with hip hop's claims to authenticity. There is the famous case of the Sugar Hill Gang "borrowing" rhymes directly from the rhyme book of Grandmaster Caz. Some performers are notorious for not writing their rhymes—and unapologetic about it as well. Diddy once wrote the check to the person who penned this line for him: "Don't worry if I write rhymes / I write checks."

But what does rap have to fear by openly acknowledging the difference between songwriter and performer? Does it still matter to rap's audience that the illusion of the inviolable MC persists, or have we come to a place where we are comfortable with the concept that some people are good poets, some good performers, and only a few are both?

In 2006 rap legend Chuck D asked the West Coast rapper Paris to pen almost all the lyrics for Public Enemy's *Rebirth of a Nation*. What was so surprising about this was how openly the two of them discussed their collaboration. Perhaps most shocking of all to the rap fan, it wasn't some rap dilettante like Shaquille O'Neal buying himself some hot lines he couldn't possibly have written himself, it was one of rap's most respected lyricists, one of its most memorable voices. Why would the man who had written the lyrics for "Yo! Bum Rush the Show" and "Fight the Power" need a ghostwriter? The answer, to hear Chuck himself explain it, was that he didn't need one, he wanted one. "I really pride myself on being a vocalist, so why can't I vocalize somebody else's writings?" he asks. He argues for rap to recognize openly what it already concedes in private. "I think often that the mistake made in rap music is that people feel that a vocalist should write their own lyrics," he says. "That's been a major, major mistake in hip-hop, because not everyone is equipped to be a lyricist and not everyone is equipped to be a vocalist."

Keep in mind that Chuck D is making this point in the midst of a long and illustrious rap career during which he has written many, many lyrics and turned in some of rap's most indelible performances. He certainly has the authority to say it, but he does so at a time when, as a senior statesman, his influence on rap itself is limited. But what if rap did follow Chuck's lead? What would it look like? Perhaps someday not far from now rap will produce its Irving Berlin, an artist famous for writing classic lyrics while never performing them himself. But for now rap still relies on the close association, at least on the surface, of creator and performer.

Rap lyrics are so closely bound to the image and identity of the performer that the very idea of a distinction seems counterintuitive. We assume that the writer is also the performer, that the lyricist and the rapper are one and the same. It has always been this way. Perhaps it is rap's proximity to literary poetry, perhaps it is the assumption of reality behind the lyrics, perhaps it's the illusion of spontaneity, but rap is inherently associated with personal expression rather than song craft. Part of the unspoken pact between MC and audience is that the MC is authentic, that what he or she is saying is sincere or real.

This is quite different from the understanding other pop artists have with their audiences. When Mariah Carey performs a song, we understand that the words she sings may or may not be her own; it makes little difference to us either way. The songs themselves, which are often undistinguished pop confections, matter less to us than the memorable performance she gives them. *American Idol* has made a franchise out of discovering popular performers who explicitly *do not* compose the songs they sing and often succeed in spite of, not because of, the material they're asked to perform.

Rap's emphasis on originality, ownership, and spontaneity so thoroughly governs the art form that even in those instances when the MC is expected to repeat previously written rhymes—at a concert, for instance—he must still find ways of maintaining the illusion of immediacy. This might mean flipping a few freestyle references into the established rhyme, or involving the audience by leaving blank spaces in the delivery for the crowd to fill in the words, or giving microphones to a crew so that they can ad-lib or emphasize particular words or phrases. All of these techniques achieve the same effect, which is to defamiliarize the live performance from the prerecorded one, in effect making it new, and thus real, again. It reestablishes the MC's relation to words. The MC is not simply a performer, but something more: an artist conceiving the lyrics before our very eyes. Of course, sometimes this comes as a detriment to the performance. Too many people on stage with mics leads to muddied sound and garbled lyrics; too much crowd participation ends up seeming like laziness on the MC's part; too much freestyle from an MC unskilled in the art can lead to disaster and embarrassment. But even when these things go wrong, they still achieve the goal of connecting MCs with their creations anew.

Style is finally the means by which MCs call attention to themselves—to their relation to other artists, to their connection to particular places or times, and perhaps most of all, to their individual excellence. But style is also a vessel, a container waiting to be filled with emotions, ideas, and stories. It is here, where rap's form meets its function, that hip-hop poetics achieves its highest calling. Ralph Ellison once said, "We tell ourselves our individual stories so that we may understand the collective." If this is true, then we have much to learn from listening to hip hop, a form uniquely suited to the art of storytelling.

FIVE **Storytelling**

STORYTELLING DISTINGUISHES RAP from other forms of popular music. That isn't to suggest that lyricists in other musical genres don't tell captivating stories: anyone who's ever heard the Eagles' "Hotel California" or Don McLean's "American Pie" or the Charlie Daniels Band's "The Devil Went Down to Georgia" knows better than that. Rap isn't even the first musical genre to tell a story to music in rapid phrases that are as close to speech as to song; that distinction belongs to operatic recitatives, which date from the seventeenth century. Rap's difference from other genres is one of degree, not of kind. Rap just tells so *many* stories. Indeed, it's difficult to identify a rap song that doesn't tell some kind of story in rhyme.

Storytelling highlights both the good and the bad in rap music and hip-hop culture. Advocates often cite rap's stories as proof of the music's truth-telling capacity, its prophetic voice for everyday people. Conversely, rap's critics target storytelling, particularly the explicit tales of so-called gangsta rap, as a corrupting influence on our culture, celebrating the worst excesses of violence, misogyny, and commercialism.

Most of rap's stories are neither incisive social commentaries nor thug fantasies. Like most stories throughout the history of human civilization, most of rap's stories are occasions to imagine alternate realities. To hear rap's storytelling at its best is to experience liberation from the constraints of everyday life, to be lost in the rhythm and the rhyme. Rap's greatest storytellers are among the greatest storytellers alive, staying close to the tones of common speech even as they craft innovations on narrative form. Rap's stories demand our attention not simply as entertainment, but as art. Whether it is Common weaving the classic hip-hop allegory "I Used to Love H.E.R." or Nas inverting narrative chronology in "Rewind," rap is an effective form for sophisticated narrative expression.

Between the street life and the good life is a broad expanse of human experience. Rap has its screenwriters, making Hollywood blockbusters in rhyme with sharp cuts, vivid characters, and intricate plotlines. It has its investigative reporters and conspiracy theorists, its biographers and memoirists, its True Crime authors and its mystery writers. It even has its comics and its sportswriters, its children's authors and its spiritualists. It is high concept and low brow; it has literary hacks and bona fide masters. It has all of these and more, extending an oral tradition as fundamental to human experience, as ancient and as essential, as most anything we have.

Even so-called gangsta rap, which one of its originators, Ice-T, prefers to call "reality rap" for its gritty fidelity to the everyday struggles of pimps, hos, and hustlers, is more concerned with imagining possible realities rather than simply recording experiences. The fact is, rap's realism is as much about telling stories as it is about telling truths. While "keeping it real" and "real talk" have become a part of rap's code of ethics, reality's importance to rap's lyrical artistry is more complicated. Reality may carry considerable weight when it comes to an MC's social capital, but it has less to do with the craft of writing great rhymes or telling good stories. In a 2006 interview, the Chicago-bred rapper Lupe Fiasco reflected upon the interrelatedness of storytelling, poetry, and rap.

> I come from a literary background, and I loved to tell stories. I remember freestyling stories, not in rhyme, by just coming up with things when I was a kid on the bus. But I couldn't play an instrument, so I decided to take my storytelling mind and to apply it to rap, which seemed like a natural thing. So I practiced a lot and really tried to apply the techniques I'd learned from poetry—which, of course, is the predecessor of rap—and include new things. I'd add haikus and try all wild poetic things, and I knew I'd have something different and interesting to say.

To tell a familiar narrative in a new way is the motivating impulse behind a lot of rap storytelling. With a storyteller's mind, rappers create poetic narratives with character and setting; conflict, climax, and resolution. They do all of this while rhyming many of their words, and usually in less than four minutes.

Rap's early years were filled with rhymed stories. Few hip-hop heads could forget Wonder Mike's question from his last verse on "Rapper's Delight": "Have you ever went over to a friend's house to eat / and the food just ain't no good?" On the other end of the spectrum from the Sugar Hill Gang's comic tone, Grandmaster Flash and the Furious Five's "The Message" offers a powerful description of urban plight: "A child is born with no state of mind / blind to the ways of mankind."

Undoubtedly the most influential storyteller in rap history is the Ruler, Slick Rick. During rap's first decade, Slick Rick helped establish the conventions that would define rap as a storytelling genre. Storytelling for him wasn't just about entertainment; he understood the expressive power of a story well told: "Stories can teach, and stories can destroy, and stories can ease tensions," he once observed. His best-known tales, love stories like "Mona Lisa," cautionary tales like "Children's Story," and explicit stories like "Sleazy Gynecologist," offer a primer of rap storytelling. Speaking of his classic album, *The Great Adventures of Slick Rick,* he recalls: "It was almost like a diary: 'When I was nineteen, this is what happened and this is what I learned from it.' It's all just writing down life experiences as you go on. I just put them in rap form."

MCs like Slick Rick put their lives, real and imagined, in rap form. Rap stories can take up anything from a few bars to an entire song, or even multiple songs. They can be told by one rapper or by several. They can follow conventional narrative chronology or be presented backwards or in fragments. They can represent a kind of rap realism or they can be fashioned as a form of heightened reality through extended metaphors or other nonliteral representations. At their best, they allow their listeners to inhabit other voices, other selves, and in the process conceive new visions of possibility and freedom.

Rappers face the same challenge as earlier poetic storytellers: Namely, how do you tell the story you want to tell the way you want to tell it while satisfying the audience's expectation of rhyme? Rhyme, along with rhythm and wordplay, makes meaning in rap's stories. Together, rap's formal qualities shape narrative structure even as they are shaped to fit narrative. The most basic convention in rap storytelling is the necessity of working within limitations, turning them to the MC's specific purposes. On "Regiments of Steel" Chubb Rock rhymes that "Rap has developed in the Motherland by storytellers / of wisdom, no wonder we're best sellers / The art was passed on from generation to generation / Developed in the mind, cause the rhyme."

The fact that rappers tell their stories in rhyme shapes their very development. Rhyme provides rap's stories with their greatest formal constraint and their most valuable literary asset. Overdetermined rhymes are the bugaboo of narrative poetry; at the same time, rhyme skillfully rendered is rap's most fundamental claim to art. Those who see no difference between a newspaper account of a crime and a rhyme about a crime fail to understand the process of artistic creation—the necessary act of imagination it takes to tell a story, any story, in verse.

Rap shares most of the rest of its basic storytelling conventions with other narrative forms, poetic and otherwise. In a rap narrative, chronology usually moves from beginning to middle to end. It most often presents an initial situation followed by a sequence of events that leads to a change or reversal, culminating in a revelation of insight enabled by that reversal. It puts characters in relation to one another; for rap this usually means the first-person narrator in relation to others who sometimes are given voice as well—either through indirect quotation or through the introduction of another (or several other) MCs. Finally, it involves patterning of formal and thematic elements that support and extend the narrative action. All of these conventions are open to revision and even rejection. The one inviolate element of rap storytelling, however, is voice.

Voice in storytelling is the governing authorial intelligence of a narrative. Voice would seem to be a given in rap: the MC and speaker's voice are one and the same. We assume that MCs are rapping to us in their own voices and, as such, that what they say is true to their own experience. All along, however, MCs have been taking far greater liberties with voice than their public stances of authenticity would suggest. Rap becomes much more interesting as poetry and rappers become more impressive as poets when we acknowledge rap as a kind of performance art, a blend of fact and fantasy, narrative and drama expressed in storytelling.

Storytelling is, at its base, a form of communication between artist and audience. Its vehicle of expression is voice. Voice is, of course, the physical instrument of expression, the sound we hear when an MC is rapping. It is also the term that defines the perspective poets take in relation to their audience. Used in this sense, a given rapper might employ multiple "voices," even in a single song. T. S. Eliot distinguished three possible voices in poetic narrative:

The first is the poet talking to himself—or to nobody. The second is the voice of the poet addressing an audience, whether large or small. The third is the voice of the poet when he attempts to create a dramatic character speaking in verse; when he is saying, not what he would say in his own person, but only what he can say within the limits of one imaginary character addressing another imaginary character.

Rap rarely employs the first voice, the cosseted tone of a poet addressing him- or herself in isolation. When they do use it, it can have powerful effects, as when Nas reflects upon his own life, or when Biggie contemplates his own death. The second and third voices, the narrative and the dramatic, are both common in rap. The narrative voice is that of the MC directly addressing an audience—this is by far the most prevalent voice, employed in braggadocio and battle raps. The dramatic voice, by contrast, uses the persona of a constructed character to address an audience (or another constructed character in the rhyme).

Narrative and dramatic voices often interpenetrate in rap. The consequence of this fusion is that audiences often don't know what to make of the rapper's poetic voice. Is the "I" speaking to them simply a narrator relating his lived experience, or is it a character in a poetic drama the rapper imagines for us? As a genre, rap has found great artistic success in having it both ways; but it has come at a social cost.

Rap most often combines the intimacy of the narrative voice with the imaginative freedom of the dramatic voice. It shares this impulse with the tall tale of the oral tradition. As an audience we have yet to condition ourselves to understand rap's tall tales as acts of projection. Rap's relation to reality is like an inside joke that much of the listening public doesn't get. The joke lies in the MC's winking assertion of the "truth" of obvious fictions. Taken to the extreme, like in the short-lived "horrorcore" rap genre in which rappers like the Gravediggaz (a group that included both the RZA and Prince Paul) described macabre tales to rival the dark imaginings of Edgar Allan Poe, this interplay is obvious to all but the most obtuse listener. But rap usually resides in the indeterminacy found in between the narrative and the dramatic voice.

As a narrative form, rap can be usefully compared to the dramatic monologue. Dramatic monologues are "poems spoken by a character through a persona (Greek for 'mask'), rather than by the poet or an unidentified speaker." Think of Marshall Mathers rapping as Eminem rapping as Slim Shady, for instance, or Troy Donald Jamerson rapping as Pharoahe Monch. "On 99 percent of the songs that I do," Pharoahe explains, "I take on a presence or a character." This is far from unusual in rap. So where does the poet's direct expression end and the persona begin? Answering this rests upon how we interpret the "I" in rap.

The dramatic monologue is most often associated with the Victorian poets. Robert Browning's poems like *My Last Duchess* and *Fra Lippo Lippi* offer powerful first-person poetic narratives that illustrate the speaker's descent into madness. In their poetic voice, they involve both the subjectivity of the "I" as poet and persona as well as the element of impersonation— of rendering, often to the point of exaggeration, the characteristic vocal qualities of another. This is precisely what we see happening when Eminem raps as Slim Shady. The voice takes on a nasally whine, the flow becomes ecstatic and erratic, all while the lyrics describe exaggerated and comic acts of violence.

Dramatic monologues extend MCs' first-person narrative voices, freeing them to say things they might not say in their own voice and explore territories of experience they might not otherwise visit were it not for the liberation of imaginative distance. MCs have written rhymes that leave their persona incarcerated (Ice Cube's "My Summer Vacation") or even dead (Cube's "Alive on Arrival" or Nas's "Undying Love")—a host of circumstances that the MC might not, or even could not, have the firsthand experience to describe.

In its use of dramatic monologue rap extends a tradition with deep roots in African-American expressive culture. The dramatic monologue is the model upon which such aspects of the oral tradition like the toasts and the stories of John Henry and Stagolee emerge. "In both Stagolee and the dramatic monologue," notes Cecil Brown, "the narrator creates a character who gives the audience a look into his special world. The audience sees through the eyes of the character the rapper creates. It is the 'I' that makes the bridge between the 'I' of the rapper and the 'I' of the character."

By severing—or at least loosening—the bond between personal identity and first-person narration, rappers find a new expressive range for their rhymes. Occasionally, rappers have gone so far as to relinquish the "I" entirely as the focal point of the lyrics. The effect is to demand that the listener understand as fiction the story contained in the lyrics. Rapping in the third person, while certainly uncommon, forces listeners to acknowledge the constructedness of the narrative. Common's "Testify" does precisely this, rendering a taut story of deception and betrayal while staying entirely in the third person. By relinquishing the first-person focus on the narrative, Common establishes a new relationship with his audience as equal bystanders in a drama of his own creation.

More common are those instances in which the MC retains the first-person voice, but retreats to the peripheries as a first-person narrator of other characters' actions. This highlights the rapper's role as storyteller even as it retains a direct connection between the story and the teller, the teller and the audience. Tupac's "Brenda's Got a Baby," Nas's "Sekou Story," and Slick Rick's "Children's Story" all come to mind. The "I" of the MC becomes the eyes of the audience, revealing a host of experiences both real and imagined.

But how do rappers see themselves in relation to the stories they tell? Do they self-consciously assert the dramatic, the fictional element, of the their storytelling? The question of authenticity in rap is phrased as a question of sincerity in literary poetry: "It may be of great interest to discover how accurately a poem reflects its author's experience, attitudes, or beliefs; but this is a question that belongs to biography not to criticism." Testifying before a Congressional subcommittee on profanity in rap in 2007, David Banner made a clear and compelling case for rap's respect as a dramatic medium: "The same respect is often not extended to hip-hop artists as to those in other arenas. Stephen King and Steven Spielberg are renowned for their horrific creations. These movies are embraced as art. Why then is our content not merely deemed horror music?"

One could answer Banner's question any number of ways. Perhaps it is a matter of racial, generational, and socioeconomic bias. Perhaps the difference is formal, having to do with the relation between creator and creation, the speaker and the spoken. Rap, after all, relies upon a near collapse of the distinction, while the other forms keep them clearly separate. Perhaps the best response comes from Jay-Z. He addresses in broad terms the very question taken up at the Congressional hearing: the perceived virulence of rap as an influence on popular culture. His answer gets to the bottom of the question of the "real" in rap.

> In hip-hop, the whole "keep it real" has become more than a phrase. Scorsese and Denzel are not tied to the films they make, so people see the separation between art and life. Unfortunately, they don't see that separation between Shawn Carter and Jay-Z. As far as they're concerned, everything I talk about is happening for real. To them, at no point is it entertainment. Rappers in general, THEY ARE the guys telling their story. To me, real is just the basis for a great fantasy. Not everything I say in a song is true. I'll take a small thing from life and build upon it, and usually it becomes a fantastic story.

Hip-hop storytelling is what happens when elements of the real become a "fantastic story." Devin the Dude echoes Jay-Z's point about fact and fiction, playfully dividing the sources of his storytelling down by percentage: "I'd say 60 percent is really just personal shit I went through; 20 percent is stuff I know about somebody who's close, or a story I heard. Ten percent is wishful thinking. And the other 10 percent is some high shit we just thought of [Laughs.]." Regardless of how it breaks down, rap storytelling is the vernacular product drawn from multiple sources—fact, fiction, and everything in between.

If we understand rap simply as fact—as it would seem many Americans do—then it's no wonder that so many are scandalized by it. But if we treat it as fantasy, as entertainment, then its offensiveness becomes indistinguishable from that of other explicit material that those very same Americans who criticize rap seem to have a voracious appetite for consuming when it comes in the form of movies or television, books or graphic novels. Rap's difference from these other forms is not one of substance but of rhetoric, not of content but of packaging. That packaging is both the product of corporate media and the stuff of the artists themselves.

Unlike writers or filmmakers, rappers rely upon the assumption of first-hand experience with their subject matter. Some have called attention to the irony of the rapper who finds fortune and fame by rapping about already having fortune and fame. Rap relies upon this slippage. "Others talk about it while I live it" is a common boast. Both artist and audience consciously create this illusion and tacitly agree to overlook its artificiality. But this fiction has a way of intruding upon fact, be it through acts of actual violence by concertgoers at rap shows—a problem that almost doomed the rap-concert business in the 1990s—to the artists themselves trying to live up to their own lyrics.

As a result, some of rap's greatest fictions have become "facts" in the public consciousness. Audiences tend to accept uncritically what rappers say as the truth. Even rappers themselves sometimes buy into their own fictions. When Tupac Shakur was in high school he wasn't gangbanging, he was in the drama club. He didn't have a criminal record until *after* he constructed the Thug Life persona that both he and his fans came to see as "real." It is a credit to Tupac as an artist that he rendered such a vivid character in rhyme that people could mistake it for the truth, and yet that identification may have cost him his life. Rarely are the stakes of rap storytelling as high as they were for Tupac, and yet almost every story rappers tell plays upon the line that divides fantasy from reality.

Undoubtedly the themes of sex and violence are disproportionately represented in rap. This seemingly impoverished range of subjects, however, has produced stories of exquisite complexity and nuance. The theme of a story is also an occasion for expression, a way of making new meanings out of familiar circumstances.

In the mid-1990s, perhaps the dominant narrative voice belonged to its dominant MC, the Notorious B.I.G., who weaved tales of gangster excess drawn more from films like *Scarface, Bad Lieutenant,* and *King of New York,* than personal experience. What makes Biggie's stories stand out is his genius in pacing, and his ability to match violence with rueful comedy. "I Got a Story to Tell," from *Life After Death,* the last album completed in his lifetime, released just two weeks after his death, shows him at the height of his creative powers. To a spare beat set by a wicked kick and snare he rhymes of a dangerous liaison with another man's woman.

What begins as a tale of sexual adventure quickly becomes one of ingenuity as the satisfied couple ("She came twice, I came last / Roll a grass"), resting in the bed of the absent cuckold—a player from the New York Knicks—is interrupted by the door opening downstairs. While the woman panics, Big stays calm ("She don't know I'm cool as a fan / Gat in hand, I don't want to blast her man / But I can and I will, though"), and directs her to stall him while he disguises himself for an ambush. When the player comes upstairs, Biggie is waiting, gun drawn and scarf around his face, ordering the man to give him all his money. Not only, Biggie tells us, does he leave with $100,000 in cash, but also with the knowledge that he has duped the man into seeing an unlikely robbery in place of a dangerous liaison. Triumphant, Biggie concludes: "Grab the keys to the five, call my niggas on the cell, / Bring some weed, I got a story to tell." The verse clocks in at less than three minutes, but the track continues for an additional minute and a half as Biggie tells the story *again* to his boys, this time talking instead of rhyming. By amplifying what was already a dramatic narrative, Biggie has, in effect, enshrined his own verse in legend.

"I Got a Story to Tell" differs in its tone from the other notable story rap on *Life After Death,* "Niggas Bleed." Gone are the playfulness and mischief, replaced by a dead-serious story about crime and consequence. Biggie's voice is not exactly his own, and yet it is informed by his rap persona. He tells the story of a drug deal gone bad. But even on this dark song, Biggie can't resist himself. With the last line, he undercuts the mood of menace by having his story end on a blunder—the getaway car hits a hydrant. This small detail transforms the entire song, with all its menace and drama, into a setup for a Biggie punch line. Unlike so many of those rappers who followed his lead, Biggie never took himself too seriously.

Perhaps the most natural story of all is the story of oneself. For rap music, this often means combining the dual modes of braggadocio and narrative into a kind of autobiography of greatness. Stories of one's rise to the top—in the rap game, in the crack game, whatever—are quite common. Stories of the MC's life form one of the core narratives in rap. Of course writing of one's own birth is a hoary conceit in Western literature, so much so that even its parodies (Laurence

Sterne's *Tristram Shandy* being foremost) are now canonical. In the African-American tradition, autobiography's roots are in the slave narratives, which almost invariably began with some version of "I was born. . . ."

MCs have employed this convention in surprising ways. A partial catalogue of birth narratives includes Ras Kass's "Ordo Abchao (Order Out of Chaos)"; the Notorious B.I.G.'s "Intro" from his debut album, *Ready to Die*; Andre 3000's "She's Alive" from *The Love Below*; and Jay-Z's "December 4th" from *The Black Album*. By far the most arresting example, though, is Nas's "Fetus," the hidden track on 2002's *The Lost Tapes*. The song begins with pensive guitar chords followed by the sound of bubbling liquid, soon overlaid with a beat and a piano riff that picks up on the guitar's melody. Then Nas begins, almost as a preface, in a tone more spoken than rapped, "Yeah. I want all my niggas to come journey with me / My name is Nas, and the year is 1973 / The beginning of me / Therefore I can see / Through my belly button window / Who I am." By endowing the insensible with voice, he aspires to an expressive level that transcends speaking for oneself, or of oneself, to one that self-consciously constructs itself as an artist giving shape to that which lacks coherence.

Another unforgettable, unconventional example of rap autobiography is Andre 3000's "A Life in the Day of Benjamin André (Incomplete)," the last track on *The Love Below*. At just over five minutes, it's a long song by today's rap standards. But what makes it stand out is the fact that he rhymes for the entire time—no hooks, no breaks, just words. Unlike the previous examples, Andre chooses to begin not with his actual birth, but his birth as a lover and as an artist: "I met you in a club in Atlanta, Georgia / Said me and homeboy

were comin' out with an album." The narrative that follows
intertwines Andre's rise to prominence as an artist with his
love relationships, most notably the tumultuous one he had
with the R&B singer Erykah Badu. The lines that follow
epitomize the way Andre balances the improvisational qualities of storytelling with a clear and directed narrative trajec-
tory, stream-of-consciousness forays with factual assertion:

> Now you know her as Erykah "On and On" Badu,
> Call "Tyrone" on the phone "Why you
> Do that girl like that, boy; you ought to be ashamed!"
> The song wasn't about me and that ain't my name.
> We're young, in love, in short we had fun.
> No regrets no abortion, had a son
> By the name of Seven, and he's five
> By the time I do this mix, he'll probably be six
> You do the arithmetic; me do the language arts
> Y'all stand against the wall blindfolded, me throw the
> > darts . . .

These lines show Andre using stark enjambment, other
voices, layered rhyme, and playful wordplay to render an unforgettable story, which also happens to be the story of his life.

Like so many other narrative forms today, rap too has
seen a revolution in its storytelling structure. In particular,
MCs have begun to devise nonlinear narratives, perhaps in
emulation of filmmakers. "Narrative is a verbal presentation
of a sequence of events or facts . . . whose disposition in time
implies causal connection and point," notes the *Princeton
Encyclopedia of Poetry and Poetics*. Obvious examples include
Nas's "Rewind," which begins with an invocation:

Listen up gangstas and honeys with your hair done
Pull up a chair, hon', and put it in the air, son
Dog, whatever they call you, god, just listen
I spit a story backwards, it starts at the ending . . .

The first image Nas describes is of a man with a bullet
coming out of his body. As we rewind, Nas inverts narrative
tension without compromising its effect upon the listener;
just the opposite, emotions are amplified. Nas uses a similar
narrative conceit on "Blaze a 50," except instead of telling
the entire story in reverse, he narrates his story in conventional fashion all the way through, but, not being satisfied
with the ending, "rewinds" to an earlier point and ends it another way.

Nas is perhaps contemporary rap's greatest innovator in
storytelling. His catalog includes songs narrated before birth
("Fetus") and after death ("Amongst Kings"), biographies
("U.B.R. [Unauthorized Biography of Rakim]") and auto-
biographies ("Doo Rags"), allegorical tales ("Money Is My
Bitch") and epistolary ones ("One Love"), he's rapped in the
voice of a woman ("Sekou Story") and even of a gun ("I
Gave You Power").

His most arresting story, however, may be "Undying
Love," a dramatic monologue about infidelity, jealousy, murder, and suicide that would have made Robert Browning
proud. It pairs well with Biggie's "I Got a Story to Tell," except where Biggie rhymes in the voice of the man cheating,
Nas rhymes in the voice of the man being cheated upon.
What's remarkable about the story this song tells is that it
pierces the armor of invincibility surrounding the MC's ego,
if only in fiction rather than fact. In the process, Nas explores

a texture of emotion rarely acknowledged in rap: human frailty. In doing so, he suggests that rap may yet be capable of encompassing the full range of human emotion.

Rap has always expressed a broad expanse of moods. Its rawest emotions are often on display when MCs aren't telling stories at all. After all, rap is the product of two seemingly disparate places—the block party and the lyrical battlefield. The good-times spirit that rap often displays is tempered by the more aggressive, even menacing, tone it takes on other occasions. As a consequence, rap is often misunderstood, taken either as a joke or as a threat. In reality it is both and so much more. It is to rap's complicated, sometimes contradictory, spirit that we now turn.

TWO COMPETITORS FACE one another, encircled by a crowd. One of them begins delivering improvised poetic lines filled with insults and puns. The second responds, trying to outdo his adversary by conjuring up even sharper verbal jabs. This goes on for several rounds until one of them gets tripped up in his words, or until the audience asserts its judgment with cheers or jeers. Such a battle could be happening right now in a Brooklyn basement or at a Bronx block party, at an open-mic night or in a street-corner cipher. It also could have happened three millennia ago, at a poetry contest in ancient Greece.

The Greeks may not have been rappers, but they certainly knew how to put on a freestyle battle. The Greek tradition of "capping" involved contests between two or more poets matching verses on set themes, responding to one another "by varying, punning, riddling, or cleverly modifying" that particular theme. Like today's freestyle rap battles between rappers, these ancient poetic competitions were largely improvised. As classical scholar Derek Collins explains, "The ability of the live performer to cap his adversary with a verse . . . while keeping in step with theme and meter at hand and at the same time producing puns, riddles, ridicule, depends among other things upon improvisation." As with rap battles, the competitive spirit of these Greek rhyme contests sometimes spilled over into physical violence. "Improvisation and humor at the wrong time," Collins writes, "occasionally resulted in death, while such repartee at the right moment could absolve one from punishable offense." It doesn't get any realer than that.

Battles are an essential part of almost every poetic tradition in the world. In the tenth-century Japanese royal court, for instance, a poet named Fujiwara no Kintô gained fame for his ability to vanquish his adversaries with just a few lines. Across the African continent, poetic contests have long been common, serving both functional and ceremonial purposes. Among the women of Namibia, for instance, a tradition of heated poetic exchange in response to perceived slights developed, a practice that continues to this day. Unifying all of these disparate traditions are the basic elements of improvisation, insult, braggadocio, and eloquence.

While battling might not be the first thing one thinks of when it comes to poetry, traditions of poetic expression around the world are rooted in it. Rap takes its rightful place within this longstanding practice of verbal warfare. When Jay-Z announced his short-lived retirement, he underscored the centrality of the battle to rap in the following public statement: "People compare rap to other genres of music, like jazz or rock 'n' roll. But it's really most like a sport. Boxing to be exact. The stamina, the one-man army, the combat aspect of it, the ring, the stage, and the fact that boxers never quit when they should." Far from disqualifying rap as a poetic form, rap's combative nature actually binds it more securely to the spirit of competition at the heart of some of the earliest poetic expressions. Whether in a freestyle session or in a recording booth, rap seems almost to require this spirit of competition.

The battle in rap is not simply between competitors, it is also between the MC and the words themselves. Mastering language before it masters you is the first contest an MC must win, even before the real competition begins. Lil Wayne, who, like Jay-Z, the MC to whom he's most often compared, claims never to write down his rhymes, picks up on this same pugilistic sensibility, but in relation to language itself. "I don't write, homie," he explains. "I just go straight in [the recording booth] and cut the music on. . . . It's sort of like a fight, I just start fightin' with the words. I don't need a tablet [of paper]. If I had a tablet, I'd get beat up."

Rap's proving ground is the cipher, a competitive and collaborative space created when MCs gather to exchange verses, either in freestyle battles or in collaborative lyrical brainstorming sessions. The cipher is a verbal cutting contest that prizes wit and wordplay above all else. It is, of course, connected to the poetic compositions born in the MC's book of rhymes, and yet it exercises its own distinct set of skills. Often a rapper is good at writing, but not at freestyling, or vice versa. It is almost an unwritten rap rule that the dopest freestylers tend to make the wackest studio albums. Within the hip-hop community, some insist that freestyling is a necessary element of MCing, while others recognize it as a completely separate skill.

Lil Wayne, as mentioned above, sees writing as an impediment to rap. "I could be at my happiest moment," he says, "my saddest moment, I could be speechless, I could be voiceless, but I could still rap. That's what I do. So that's why I really don't use the pen and pad, 'cause I kind of feel like when you use the pen and pad, you're readin', And when you're readin' somethin', man, you're payin' attention to what you're readin' instead of what you're doin'." So what is freestyle's relation to rap's poetry? After all, the complex poetics we've been discussing thus far are most often the product of composition and revision, not just unfiltered impromptu expression. Is freestyling, therefore, somehow less "poetic" than those lines born in an MC's book of rhymes? Are the lyrical products of each necessarily distinct?

Most MCs tend to underscore the connection rather than the division between freestyling and writing rhymes. "When you write a rhyme it arrives in the form of a freestyle anyway," observes Guru. "It's just a matter of how you catch it and capture it and put it down on paper." Black Thought of the Roots similarly suggests an inherent connection between the two methods of lyrical creation. Speaking about "Proceed," a classic track from an early album, he remarks: "All the lyrics on there were written down, not freestyled. But when I wrote the stuff down, it was also always the first thing that came into my head. So I guess it was half and half." Kurupt echoes both MCs when he describes his own compositional process as a hybrid of the written and the freestyled, working in symbiotic unity:

> I think in freestyle, I'll kick a rhyme right now, you see what I'm saying? That's like my whole thing. That's where I get my rhymes from. I might freestyle and say something that I just think is so catty. So then I just sit down and write the freestyle rhyme I said, but then I calculate it more, you see what I'm saying? I put more brain power to it when I just sit and write it because I can think more about how I can word it, you see what I'm saying?

No matter how we define the precise connection, the freestyle battle provides a way of understanding something of the spirit of rap poetry as a whole. Most rap, whether freestyled or written, celebrates individual excellence. Through ritualized insults made up of puns and other plays on words, rap embodies a spirit of competition, even when no competitors are in sight. Understanding the rap battle helps explain why MCs often rail against unnamed "sucker MCs," even if they're rapping alone in the recording booth. It doesn't really matter if LL had someone specific in mind when he wrote, "LL Cool J is hard as hell / Battle anybody I don't care who you tell / I excel, they all fail / I'm gonna crack shells, Double-L must rock the bells." The lines are just as fierce, the swagger just as hard. Competition is abstract, but no less real. Whether freestyled or written, something in rap requires this spirit of verbal combat. It is rap's motivating energy and its sustaining drive.

Rap was born in the first person. It is a music obsessed with the "I," even to the point of narcissism. MCs become larger than life through rhyme, often projecting images of impervious strength. The flipside, of course, is vulnerability, something one sees only rarely, but which is powerful when it appears. When rappers talk about themselves, there is more at stake than the individual. Through self-exploration, they expose an expanse of meaning.

This chapter is about what MCs rhyme about when they aren't telling lengthy stories—in other words, what MCs rhyme about most of the time. While this includes innumerable topics, we can summarize them in just a few: celebrating themselves, dissing their opponents, and shit-talking in every other possible way. This form of lyrical celebration of self and denigration of others can be puerile, but it can also be gratifying. It is fueled by one of rap's great intangible and essential qualities: *swagger*. Swagger, or just *swag*, is the essential quality of lyrical confidence. It expresses itself in an MC's vocal delivery, in confidence and even brashness. Swagger is difficult to describe, but you know it when you hear it. You can hear it in these lines from Lil Wayne's "Dr. Carter,"

> And I don't rap fast, I rap slow
> 'Cause I mean every letter in the words in the sentence of
>   my quotes.
> Swagger just flow sweeter than honey oats.
> That swagger, I got it, I wear it like a coat.

Wayne displays the very swagger he's rhyming about in his deliberate meaning and assured ownership ("That swagger, I got it . . ."). Swagger is not new to rap, of course. It has its roots in the African-American verbal practice of signifying.

Over centuries, black expressive culture has developed a tradition called signifying. Signifying is a rhetorical practice that involves repetition and difference, besting and boasting. As Henry Louis Gates, Jr., wrote in his groundbreaking study *The Signifying Monkey*, signifying is "the rhetorical principle in Afro-American vernacular discourse" with roots that stretch through slavery back to West Africa. Among black Americans, signifying has taken on many forms over the years. The dozens, familiar to many through "Yo Mama" jokes, involves a ritualized exchange of insults, with the winner being the one who could marshal creativity without breaking cool. Another product of the signifying tradition was the toasts, long narrative poems often recited by black men in barbershops, on street corners, and in penitentiaries. The toasts detailed the exploits of street hustlers and outlaw heroes like the signifying monkey and Shine. As in so many of today's raps, in the toasts the underdog almost always ended up on top.

In the decade before hip hop was born, the toasts and other "raps" gained great popularity. Artists like Gil Scott-Heron and the Last Poets and other masters of signifying like Muhammad Ali and H. Rap Brown are often mentioned as forefathers of rap. Certainly they deserve credit as major influences—sometimes even direct influences, particularly in rap's early years. H. Rap Brown's famous "Rap's Poem" from the 1960s might easily be mistaken for a rap verse with its profane braggadocio:

> I'm the bed tucker the cock plucker the motherfucker
> The milkshaker the record breaker the population maker

> The gun-slinger the baby bringer
> The hum-dinger the pussy ringer
> The man with the terrible middle finger.
> The hard hitter the bullshitter the polynussy getter
> The beast from the East the Judge the sludge
> The women's pet the men's fret and the punks' pin-up boy.
> They call me Rap the dicker the ass kicker
> The cherry picker the city slicker the titty licker

Brown was employing the rhetorical figure kenning, popularized a few millennia ago in *Beowulf*, which joins two terms together to form an eponym, a self-descriptive alias. It's impossible not to hear echoes of Rap Brown in GZA when he rhymes "I be the body-dropper, the heartbeat-stopper / child-educator plus head-amputator." Perhaps the classic example of rap kenning, though, is Smoothe da Hustler and Trigga Tha Gambler trading bars on 1995's "Broken Language." Spitting their brand of thugged-out linguistics, they deliver fierce lines like these:

> (Smoothe)
> The coke cooker, the hook up on your hooker hooker
> the 35 cents short send my 25's over looker
> (Trigga)
> The rap burner, the Ike the Tina Turner
> ass whippin' learner, the hitman, the money earner
> (Smoothe)
> The -tologist without the derma-
> me and my little brother
> (Trigga)
> The cock me back, bust me off nigga

The undercover
Glock to your head pursuer

It is a testament to the staying power of the technique as well as to the skill of Smoothe and Trigga's use of it that Redman and Method Man remade the track in 2008. This kind of self-mythologizing is a common means of braggadocio, exalting the individual by making him or her too big for one name alone. It is an ancient signifying technique that seems as fresh as ever.

Rap Brown's influence is even more apparent in hip hop's first commercial hit, "Rapper's Delight." In a striking example of signifying, The Sugar Hill Gang echoes Brown's precise language. In the original, Rap rhymes, "Yes, I'm hemp the demp the women's pimp / Women fight for my delight." Years later, Big Bank Hank rhymes, "Yes, I'm imp the gimp, the ladies' pimp / The women fight for my delight." Echoing across both time and genre, what unifies these two expressions is the art of signifying.

Of course, it is facile simply to draw a straight line between verbal expressions like the dozens and the toasts and rap. Rap is also music; it relies upon a rhythmic, and often a harmonic and melodic, relation to song. What rap shares with these earlier expressive practices is an attitude, a spirit of competition and drive towards eloquence. Rap wears its relation to tradition lightly, never with an onerous sense of the past. And yet the past is always there, a past that runs through Africa, but also through Europe and Asia as well. Signifying is far from dead; it is alive and well in rap. For some, that's a problem.

Rap signifying was unexpectedly held up to public scrutiny in the summer of 2008 when a clip of NBA star

Shaquille O'Neal dissing former teammate Kobe Bryant in a rap "freestyle" appeared on the celebrity gossip site TMZ.com. The lumbering lyricist dropped a series of heavy-handed put-downs only a week after Bryant's Lakers were eliminated after they lost game six of the NBA Finals by thirty-nine points to the Boston Celtics. Their personal animosity stems from both on and off the court tensions during their years as Lakers teammates, when they won three straight NBA titles. When Shaq took the mic at a New York club in late June, he channeled much of his animosity into the verse. "Check it. . . . You know how I be / Last week Kobe couldn't do it without me," Shaq begins, then meanders off on a tangent about his rhyme skills not being as good as Biggie's (obvious) and how he lives next to Diddy (or, rather, Diddy lives next to him), before returning again to Kobe. At the end of the verse he spits this bit of rap invective:

> I'm a horse . . . Kobe ratted me out
> That's why I'm getting divorced.
> He said Shaq gave a bitch a mil'
> I don't do that, 'cause my name's Shaquille.
> I love 'em, but don't leave 'em
> I got a vasectomy, now I can't breed 'em
> Kobe, how my ass taste?
> Everybody: Kobe, how my ass taste?
> Yeah, you couldn't do without me . . .

In a lyrical equivalent of kicking somebody when he's down, Shaq takes the occasion of Kobe's defeat to settle a number of scores, including getting back at Kobe for bringing Shaq's name up in an interview with police after Kobe was arrested for sexual assault in Colorado. At once, Shaq's rhyme is the best and worst example of rap signifying. Best, because it clearly displays how rap can be used effectively for the purposes of character assassination. Worst, because Shaq's limited skills as a lyricist keep the verse from achieving the subtlety and invention that signifying at its best always employs. Shaq's verse is a blunt instrument rather than a surgical knife; it doesn't cut out his opponent's heart as much as it attempts to smash it.

Kept within the confines of rap culture, it's unlikely that Shaq's performance would have garnered much notice. It was only after it spilled over into the mainstream media that it became a minor controversy. When first asked for comment, Shaq appealed to the expectations of signifying in rap, which call for an individual who's been dissed to diss back; getting mad means you've lost the battle. Speaking to ESPN's Stephen A. Smith, Shaq responded: "I was freestyling. That's all. It was all done in fun. Nothing serious whatsoever. That is what MCs do. They freestyle when called upon." The explanation of "that's what MCs do" was undoubtedly befuddling to the average viewer. And yet Shaq's appeal to the conventions of the art form, while perhaps something of a rouse, nonetheless speaks to the importance of signifying in the MC's craft. For most people unfamiliar with these conventions, however, Shaq's performance was nearly inexplicable. NPR and Fox News commentator Juan Williams responded to the incident by suggesting, quite seriously, that O'Neal seek psychological assistance. While rap's been around for decades, many still find it difficult to make sense out of dissing and braggadocio, two sides of the same signifying coin.

Dissing at its best employs as much wit as it does insult. When the Pharcyde recorded "Ya Mama" in 1992, they delivered their lyrics with playful panache and inventiveness.

> Ya mom is so fat (How fat is she?)
> Ya mama is so big and fat that she can get busy
> With twenty-two burritos, when times are rough
> I seen her in the back of Taco Bell in handcuffs.

Like in a schoolyard snap session, the group trades verses back and forth, trying to outdo each other with their originality. Listening to the track, you can hear them responding to one another's lines with laughter and appreciation. This same spirit is alive in 2008's "Lookin Boy" from the Chicago group Hotstylz featuring Yung Joc. Joc begins by introducing the track ("We gonna have a roastin' session"), then each rapper takes turns inventing disses, not at anyone in particular, but for the sheer joy of conceiving the wildest and wittiest putdowns they can. Raydio G opens the track with these lines:

> Weak lookin' boy, you slow lookin' boy,
> Dirty white sock on your toe lookin' boy,
> You rat lookin' boy,
> "Will you marry me?" Splat! lookin' boy,
> Whoopi Goldberg black lip lookin' boy,
> Midnight Train Gladys Knight lookin' boy,
> You poor lookin' boy, Don Imus ol' nappy headed ho lookin' boy

What makes these lines, and the ones that follow it, work is that they exploit stereotype, maybe even getting you to laugh at something you might not otherwise consider funny (like the Imus comment). Combining sound effects, off the wall references, and straightforward insults, the song exemplifies the range and meaning of the diss in rap signifying.

While dissing concerns someone else, *braggadocio* centers on the self. More than just bragging, braggadocio consists of MCs' verbal elevation of themselves above all others. Like the diss, braggadocio can range from the straightforward (like Miami's DJ Khaled screaming "We the best!" on most of his songs) to the more ingenious (like Los rhyming that "I'm so out of this world I make telescopes squint" on his freestyle to Lil Wayne's "A Milli").

Braggadocio is one of the most commonly misunderstood elements of rap, in part because it seems so straightforward on the surface. Play rap for someone who doesn't usually listen to the music or only listens to it casually and one of the first things you're likely to hear is: "Why are they bragging so much about themselves?" Even an otherwise astute observer of culture can end up making false assumptions about rap based upon this singular element of its boasts. I was reminded of this in 2007 when I attended a taping of Bill Maher's HBO show, *Real Time*. His guests that week included Rahm Emanuel (then–Democratic congressman from Illinois, now President Barack Obama's chief-of-staff); journalist Pete Hamill, and professor Michael Eric Dyson of Georgetown University. Maher led them, as usual, through a discussion of the week's news: Iraq; the recent racial incident in Jena, Louisiana; the 2008 presidential race. Then Bill launched into one of his trademark rants. What was unusual in this instance, however, was that the subject of his attack was hip hop.

Maher isn't a knee-jerk critic of rap. He often takes provocative, contrarian stances on many social and cultural subjects—rap included. He's a familiar face at the Playboy Mansion and, perhaps more important for hip-hop heads, he once dated Karrine Steffans, also known as Superhead, the most infamous "video vixen" in hip-hop history. His problem with rap was its braggadocio. "I'm a fan of hip hop, but I don't have kids," Maher said, "And I gotta say if I had kids would I want them to listen to a steady diet of 'I'm a P-I-M-P'? No, I wouldn't. . . . Ninety percent of it is affirmative action for the ego. Ninety percent of it is bragging, and I'm sorry, but modesty is a virtue."

In most rap modesty is anything but a virtue. But how did extolling one's own greatness take on such a vital role in rap from its earliest days? Why is braggadocio so vital to the art form? The answers are as obvious as they are insufficient: partly as a consequence of rap's birth in the battle; partly as a consequence of rap's origins in a black oral tradition that celebrates individual genius; partly as a result of the interests and attitudes of its primary creators and consumers— young men; partly as a result of it being the creation of young *black* men seeking some form of power to replace those denied them. Hip-hop historian William Jelani Cobb makes this point, "In hip hop—and inside the broken histories of black men in America—respect is the ultimate medium of exchange. And that is to say, in battling, the rapper is gambling with the most valuable commodity available: one's rep and the respect that flows from it." What Cobb elsewhere terms "the scar tissue of black male powerlessness" might be just another way of identifying Maher's "affirmative action for the ego." Both are ways of identifying a defensive, recuperative gesture and, largely, a symbolic one. But beyond seeking an explanation for *why* rappers boast, it

is equally important to understand *how* they boast. And
what rappers boast about is not always as straightforward as
many assume.

Rap is a musical form made by young men and largely
consumed by young men. It is music about those things generally on the minds of young men: sex, cars, money, and
above all, their own place in society. But rap has never been
just about this. From the beginning what made rap different
from other forms of braggadocio is that it extolled excellence
not simply in the stereotypically masculine pursuits—wealth,
physical strength, sexual prowess—but in something new: in
poetry, eloquence, and artistry. Here were young men boasting of intellectual and artistic pursuits. Just listen to a young
LL Cool J, for instance, in these famous lines from one of
rap's quintessential signifying songs, "I'm Bad":

> Never retire or put my mic on the shelf
> The baddest rapper in the history of rap itself
> Not bitter or mad, just provin' I'm bad
> You want a hit, give me a hour plus a pen and a pad.

That "hour plus a pen and a pad" is proof that LL Cool J's
badness is nothing less than a revelation. It suggests that in
hip hop, artistry is a commodity right alongside money, power,
and respect.

To understand rap's braggadocio, it is useful to look to the
birth of so-called gangsta rap. While gangsta rap came to
public attention in the late 1980s with West Coast artists
like N.W.A. and Ice-T, it is an East Coast MC, Schoolly D,
who is most often credited with pioneering the genre.
Schoolly D took as his subject urban crime on the streets of

his native Philadelphia. Long before curse words became commonplace in rap, Schoolly D routinely cussed up a storm on his albums. More than that, the subject matter he chose distinguished him from his contemporaries. While Run-DMC was rhyming about "My Adidas," Schoolly D was rapping about pimps, hos, and hustlers. This is not to say, however, that Schoolly D was somehow the first person to extol the virtues of criminal life in rhyme. The black vernacular tradition of the toasts routinely valorized outlaw characters like the pimp and the pusher. Murder and mayhem were frequent themes.

Schoolly D himself paid tribute to these earlier influences when he recorded his own version of the famous toast "The Signifying Monkey," something he called "The Signifying Rapper." "The Signifying Rapper" first appeared on Schoolly D's 1988 album *Smoke Some Kill*, and reached an even broader audience when director Abel Ferrera used the song in a climactic scene from his 1992 film *Bad Lieutenant*. Built upon a replayed riff from Led Zeppelin's "Kashmir," the song lyrically embodies the hard edge of the music. As William Eric Perkins describes it, "'Signifying Rapper' . . . is a tour de force, a kind of ghetto Brer Rabbit tale replete with gruesome violence, homophobia, and sexual perversion. . . . Schoolly D's twisted genius lies in his ability to paint a lyrical picture of inner-city decay. But his persona led other rappers to create equally hardened characters whose quirkiness was magnified in their lyrical and stylistic sophistication." After Zeppelin's Jimmy Page heard the song while watching Ferrera's film, he filed suit against Ferrera and Schoolly D. The scene was cut from the film and all remaining copies of the CD, which had been out for nearly five years, were destroyed.

Like the toasts, rap often relies upon the construction of a larger-than-life persona, an outlaw hero with superhuman aptitudes and appetites. The Notorious B.I.G. is not Christopher Wallace, 2Pac is not Tupac Shakur, although he seems to have pushed himself to live up to his persona, to his own detriment. Rappers' aliases afford them the necessary distance from their own identity to fashion alternate selves, voices that are louder and bolder, anything but their own. This is true, of course, of most artists. And yet for rap it has come to dominate the form in ways unprecedented in other genres.

Rappers create, observes music critic Kelefa Sanneh, "an outsized hero that has more sex than you're really having, that does more violence than you're really doing, that sells more drugs than you've ever sold." LL Cool J as lover. Chuck D as new Malcolm. KRS as teacher. Pac as thug poet. Biggie as lovable gangsta. "The persona overshadows the person and the person can be crushed by the persona," Nelson George remarks. Historian Robin D. G. Kelley picks up on this same point:

> Exaggerated and invented boasts of criminal acts should sometimes be regarded as part of a larger set of signifying practices. Growing out of a much older set of cultural practices, these masculinist narratives are essentially verbal duels over who is the "baddest." They are not meant as literal descriptions of violence and aggression, but connote the playful use of language itself.

Kelley's last phrase is essential. Too often we approach rap music with a startling and willful lack of imagination that we don't bring to heavy metal, for instance. The "playful use of language itself" is made apparent by artists like the Notorious B.I.G. whose self-deprecating wit was as sharp as his excoriating disses of others. It may be less apparent—but not to say more subtle—in an artist like 50 Cent whose celebration of a gangsta aesthetic and its trappings (bulletproof vests, semi-automatic handguns, bandanas tied around the mouth and neck) becomes so complete that it *almost* disguises the glamorous life he actually lives—the untold riches, VIP treatment, and award show dates with Hollywood celebrities. Yes, 50 was a small-time crack dealer for a time, but this actual experience is much farther removed from the cartel fantasies of his lyrical fictions than is the high-stakes hustling of the record executives who push him as their product. The point is that gangsta rap has always been an image, an act, and a process of signification not just with so-called studio gangstas but even with the real-life former (and occasionally even current) petty criminals who lived in the shadow of the images they create.

For those MCs able to control the image, the gangsta persona can prove a powerful means of expression. Ice-T, the godfather of gangsta rap, drew inspiration from real life even as he consciously crafted his rhymes to serve his own imaginative purposes. On songs like "Drama" and "I'm Your Pusher," he renders rhyme personas that are "real" inasmuch as they reflect what he sometimes saw in the streets, but are stylized in the way he crafts the stories to serve his art. "When my dad would teach me lessons, he would never just say: 'Don't do it,'" Ice-T explains. "He would tell me stories and he would get me into it. It would be like: 'He was about to get a million dollars, but that night he OD'd.' So I always used that technique. Because I *do* really, truly come from the game, I can't write a story about the hustle where the dude doesn't end up in prison or dead. Because all the real stories do. If I'm rhyming and I shoot somebody, I'm on the run in the next verse." In this case, reality not only lives alongside fiction, it actually shapes the terms of that fiction—demanding authenticity that leads not to glorifying the gangsta aesthetic but to representing and, ultimately, challenging it.

Rap also has a long tradition of what might be called rapping about rapping. When the act of rhyming itself becomes the subject of the rhymes, MCs turn their attention to the tools and the process of their art. Out of this we get Nas describing himself as "a poet, a preacher and a pimp with words." Such artistic self-awareness contrasts with an equally established tradition of rappers outwardly rejecting rap's poetic identity—in other words, of rapping about not needing or wanting to rap at all. This occurs when MCs either downplay their creative process or assert a counter-identity in its place. Out of this we get Malice from Clipse insisting that "I'm not a rapper," or Jay-Z asserting that "I'm not a businessman, I'm a business, man." Hustler or commodity, these are clever fictions meant to disguise the true process of the poet's work. All rappers are poets; whether they are good poets or bad poets is the only question.

At different times in rap's history it has been fashionable for MCs to project either interest or indifference in relation to their craft. After Jay-Z began boasting that he never wrote down his rhymes, or that he could compose an entire verse in fifteen minutes flat, or that he could record it in a single take, it became fashionable for other rappers to do—or at least to *say*—the same. Of course, what might be true for

Jay-Z, the self-proclaimed "Mike Jordan of Rap," does not necessarily hold for your average MC, nor, in fact, does it always hold for Jay-Z himself.

What do rappers' stand to gain by downplaying their artistry? It is in the interest of the MC to make rap seem effortless. Hip hop as a culture celebrates virtuosity, excellence that expresses itself with ease. Like b-boys executing a series of complex kinesthetic motions only to end by brushing off their shoulders with feigned indifference, MCs often boast a "Look, Ma, no hands!" lyrical aesthetic that downplays the work it takes to create the rhymes they spit. An audience listens to rap to be entertained, not to be impressed with the formal sophistication at work. The purpose of sophisticated poetics is not to call attention to itself, but to absorb itself so fully within the art that it is invisible to the naked eye—or ear. Downplaying the work they do is just one strategy MCs use, both within and without their rhymes, to maintain the necessary illusion of ease.

The tension between inspiration and craft, between the conception that great art emerges fully formed or that it is the product of conscientious labor, is a matter of great discussion and debate in almost every literary tradition in the history of the world. Aristotle mused upon it in the *Poetics*. Wordsworth and Coleridge troubled over it in their writings in the nineteenth century. What's new in rap is the commercial element. A major consequence of rap becoming a global industry is that it also attracts individuals primarily motivated by profit. Those hip-hop heads who long for a golden age of rap when the MC did it for the love must realize that the moment rhyme started to pay, or showed the potential to pay, which is to say only a few years into its existence, rap opened itself up to commercial interests.

We've reached a point in rap culture in which 50 Cent will admit to *Forbes* magazine that rhyming for him is a business decision. We've moved beyond boasts about collecting fat royalty checks to rhymes about business deals with multinational corporations. This opens up an important question for those of us interested in rap's poetics: Can rap be both good business and good poetry? Do the calculations that a rap businessman must make to account for market conditions leave any space left for the motivations of the wordsmith?

Rap's artistry, some critics argue, is in inverse proportion to its profitability. But this argument is too absolute. "Commercial success and artistic integrity are not mutually exclusive," writes Stic.man, half of dead prez. "Just because you are a starving artist does not mean that you automatically have more skills or that you lack them. And conversely, just because you are a platinum selling artist it doesn't mean you have no integrity to the roots and artistry of hip hop. . . . You must understand that artistic credibility and financial success can, should, and do work together wherever possible."

While commercialism may not have killed rap's poetry, it has certainly changed it. The influences of corporate labels and commercial radio as gatekeepers separating true MCs from their audience are obvious. Of equal importance, however, is how rap's profitability affects the MC's craft *before* distribution and radio play even become factors. What impact, in other words, does commercialism have on MCs writing in their book of rhymes?

Chuck D, for one, has decried what he calls the "rise of the culture of black animosity" that emerges when rampant commercialism meets a gotta-get-mine perspective. In many ways, rap has become the soundtrack to this cultural malady, expressed in gun claps and diss tracks. Rap at once reflects and helps create a cultural climate of black violence and black response. "I just think in general our society limits the range in which men can express their emotions. You just have to have your game face on all the time." Consequently, rap is often obsessed with image. One of the dominant rap personas consists of presenting yourself as someone worthy of respect through *physical* domination rather than through the exercise of often unattainable "virtual powers" like money and social and political standing—things historically denied to black Americans. Indeed, as is evident in an artist like 50 Cent, these modes of power sometimes converge, but always return to the base of physical domination and violence as the anchor of their strength.

This culture of animosity has been a shaping force in the thematic range of hip hop's poetry. Whether in the classic site of rap domination and submission, the battle, or in the more abstract forms of the same dynamic in so-called gangsta rap, hip hop has always drawn from these conventional masculine energies. Among the relatively few voices to challenge, or even to acknowledge this obvious impulse is the spoken-word poet Saul Williams. Williams sees a fundamental distinction between the poet and the MC, not in terms of their respective forms, but in terms of their expressive ranges. Where the MC must be in control—the "master of ceremonies"—a poet "is allowed to be introspective, allowed to raise questions," he told Salon.com in 2004. "The poet is allowed to be vulnerable whereas, with MCs and in hip-hop, vulnerability is a sign of weakness. And so it becomes less and less real, less connected to the true nature of humankind. The further we go on the tip of invulnerability and being hardcore, the less we can show a soft side."

The greatest casualty of hip hop's idea of invulnerability may be its capacity to express the full and complex range of human emotion. Rap's audience is driven by sometimes schizophrenic impulses. The aura of invulnerability attracts us with its obvious difference from ourselves. As an audience we don't simply want to see ourselves replicated, we want at least to believe that the artist before us is somehow better— elevated, enlightened, inspired, somehow closer to perfection. Rap often advances this mode of escapism. However, when an entertainer becomes not simply distanced but aloof from us and the collective human experience, this usually spells the end of their popularity. Rap has proved itself quite skilled at toeing this line, of balancing its audience's need for idols with its desire for connection. The next challenge is to see if rap can become something other than the soundtrack of adolescent rebellion, more than the music of the moment.

It has already begun. What distinguishes the rap that lasts from that which disappears isn't always only the level of technical skill. Another significant component is the expressive capacity of the lyrics. Both Tupac and Biggie shared a necessary humanism, a sense of fallibility that endeared them to their fans. Tupac's boasts were balanced by his more introspective ventures into his own mortality, social and gender issues, and his family history. Biggie's persona was so outsized that even his boasts took on a certain self-effacing comedy, one that contrasts sharply with the depth of tragedy and pain expressed elsewhere in his lyrics of suicide and self-abnegation. These artists are only the most visible examples of a set of countertraditions within rap lyricism that challenges the dominant ethos of invulnerability, the thematic of hardcore.

Rap's expressive growth is also visible from outside hip-hop culture, in the ways that rap has become a mode of expression for an unlikely array of individuals. Early in 2006, *Saturday Night Live* ran a sketch called "Lazy Sunday" in which two of its cast members, Chris Parnell and Andy Samberg, performed a two-minute parody of an old-school rap video. The clip, often referred to as "The Chronicles of Narnia Rap," quickly became an Internet phenomenon, a fixture on YouTube, inspiring numerous imitators. What made the skit so remarkable wasn't simply that Parnell and Samberg are white—white MCs have been around nearly since the beginning of rap and Eminem has gone on to become one of the most respected and successful MCs of all time. Nor was it that they had pulled off a successful rap parody—this has been done before and since; later in 2006 the king of pop parody, Weird Al Yankovic, did a sendup of Chamillionaire's "Ridin' Dirty" called "White and Nerdy." What makes "Lazy Sunday" stand out from so many of the response raps that it inspired was that Parnell and Samberg's flows, though unabashedly old school, were actually quite good. Their rhymes never seem forced, even when rhyming multisyllabically.

Rap parodies like "Lazy Sunday" or Jamie Kennedy's similarly amusing and skillful "Rollin' with Saget" work because they play upon the premise that rap is always dead serious, that even when rappers laugh, they rarely laugh at themselves. Humor emerges from the ironic distance between the "whiteness" (read: harmlessness, softness, corniness) of the white rapper and the "blackness" (read:

dangerousness, hardness, coolness) of rap itself. Tied up in this, of course, are long-standing issues of racial stereotype. These parodists achieve in rap a lesser version of what Ralph Ellison claimed the white southern novelist William Faulkner achieved in rendering black characters in his fiction: "to start with the stereotype, accept it as true, and then seek out the human truth which it hides." By playing into common assumptions about race and rap, they invite examination of the human complexity that pulses behind the mask of stereotype.

Rap's stereotypical place in the popular imagination is dominated by images of aggression: young black men talking about guns, drugs, and violence. Comedy would seem to have little place in rap. But rap has more than its share of comedians, from clown princes like Flavor Flav and Ol' Dirty Bastard to slow, sardonic wits like Too Short and Snoop Dogg. It is in that territory between fear and laughter that rap finds its most fertile expression. "I might crack a smile, but ain't a damn thing funny," Mobb Deep's Prodigy once rhymed, summing up the common attitude of mirthless menace. Even at its funniest, in the clever rhymes of the Notorious B.I.G., for instance, or the weed-head high jinx of Redman and Method Man, rap often retains an underlying promise of violence. "Rap is really funny, man," Ice-T once cautioned, "but if you don't see that it's funny, it will scare the shit out of you."

Rap's comedy is often complicit with its aggression—sometimes serving to undercut the violence even to the point of parody, other times rendering it more sinister still. Rap shares in the spirit of the tragicomic, the governing mood behind a host of black American cultural expressions, from the blues to the dozens. Rap's defining difference, though, is here: While it sometimes laughs, it rarely laughs at itself.

At its most basic level, comedy comes in three types: jokes on them, jokes on us, and jokes on me. The first form is often the lowest; it is humor mixed with a sadistic urge to cause others pain. Out of this strain we get schoolyard taunts and racist jokes. When the joke's on them, the teller need not implicate him- or herself at all. The second form, where the joke's on us, is more common and more affirming. This is the kind where the joke is shared by all or most. Think about standup comics who make their living offering witty observations; think *Seinfeld* and *The Cosby Show* where the comedy is geared toward the common human denominator of experience. The final form leaves the teller most vulnerable, and thus it should come as little surprise that it is the rarest form of all. When the joke is on the teller, the implications are personal and sometimes painful. The laughter, therefore, is deep and often cathartic. This is blues humor. This is Richard Pryor doing a bit about almost burning himself to death while freebasing cocaine. This is laughing to keep from crying.

It might be too simple to say that these three levels of comedy are in ascending relation to one another, that this final form somehow transcends the others. But I think it's safe to say that being able to find humor in one's own experience has been a source of great inspiration to some of the finest artists in a range of disciplines. Is hip hop expansive enough in its expression to encompass such vulnerability? Do the conventions of the form allow the necessary distance for artists to look back at themselves with ironic awareness? "Hip hop doesn't place as high a premium on irony as its ancestral forms, particularly blues—even as it relies upon blues and the surrounding blues folklore for much of its material," writes William Jelani Cobb. "This is not to say that hip hop

is completely anti-ironic, simply that irony is not at the center of the hip hop ethos. That said, hip hop has precious little
room for acknowledging pain in order to ultimately transcend it." Ralph Ellison's famous definition of the blues
comes to mind here: "The blues is an impulse to keep the
painful details and episodes of a brutal experience alive in
one's aching consciousness, to finger the jagged grain, and to
transcend it, not by the consolation of philosophy but by
squeezing from it a near-tragic, near-comic lyricism. As a
form, the blues is an autobiographical chronicle of personal
catastrophe expressed lyrically."

Acknowledging pain is acknowledging weakness, even if
that weakness is exposed only to transcend it with strength
and resolve. I would depart from Cobb's otherwise apt char-
acterization of rap's difference from the blues in that I believe
that rap has a tremendous capacity for lyrically expressing
pain, one that is even now emerging. The greatest art celebrates human frailty more often than it does invincibility.

Rather than decrying what rap is, it might be more fruit-
ful to consider what it can become. As a musical and poetic
form in its relative adolescence, rap is likely to undergo even
more radical changes in the years ahead. Where will those
changes lead? The greatest challenge for rap may be in finding the expressive range to deal with the complexity of human experience, in its weakness as well as in its strength.

Rap's poetry may prove its lasting legacy to global culture. When all the club bangers have faded, when all the
styles and videos are long forgotten, the words will remain.
"Timeless music. . . ," Jay-Z mused in a 2006 interview with
XXL. "Right now in hip-hop, there's a lot of disposable music, and I believe the genre will suffer unless you have an

event album." For Jay-Z, an "event album" is one that aspires
to the highest level of craft. Rather than a handful of ready-
made radio singles with filler tracks mixed in, it is an artfully
constructed album that aspires to greatness. It is Dr. Dre's
The Chronic or Jay-Z's own *The Blueprint*. It is an earthquake
that shifts the cultural topography one verse at a time.

Hip hop is haunted by this sense of tradition. It is a music whose death was announced soon after its birth, and the
continuing reports of its demise seemingly return with each
passing year. Part of the fear, as Jay-Z perceived, is that much
of the music is disposable—cultural ephemera intended to
entertain audiences for the moment, not to make a lasting
contribution to our culture. Part of it, too, is the fear of commercialization and cooption. When rappers talk about writing their verses on the spot in the studio, blunt in hand, in
fifteen minutes flat, it's hard to imagine they clutter their
minds with thoughts of tradition. Those MCs who do think
about tradition often find themselves ignored by the listening public. Mos Def is one MC who's found commercial success without compromising craft. He describes his longing for
tradition this way:

> All I know is I wanted to feel a certain way when I heard music,
> and I was making music from in me. . . . And I wanted it to be
> something that was durable. You can listen to all these Jimi
> records and Miles records and Curtis Mayfield records; I wanted
> to be able to add something to that conversation.

Rap has already found its way into the American song-
book alongside legends like Jimi Hendrix, Miles Davis, and
Curtis Mayfield. But unlike rock, jazz, and soul, rap has been
slow to gain acknowledgment as great art. That is starting to

change. Rap now constitutes a tradition unto itself, with roots in Western poetry as well as in African-American oral expression. More than thirty years after rap's birth in the South Bronx, it is now possible to talk about rap's history as well as its present. It is the focal point in a renaissance of the word, a development reshaping the very nature of our daily experience, whether we listen to it or not.

Epilogue

NOT ALL RAP is created equal. Not every rhyme responds well to close analysis. A lot of rap verses, like a lot of other poems, are fashioned with little skill or care. They might make for good music, but they're terrible poetry. When it comes to listening, however, well-crafted rhymes aren't always necessary. To paraphrase T. S. Eliot, even the most banal lyrics can seem profound when accompanied by the right music. Great pop music is rarely great poetry; the lyrics usually end up seeming shallow and saccharine when confined to the page.

Hip-hop lyrics are different in that a striking number of them *do* hold up on the page. The same musical characteristics that annoy rap's critics—the predictability of the beat, the repetitive nature of the music, and the limited melodic range—are the very qualities that make it ideal for poetry. The spareness and the repetition lend emphasis to the words.

The beat's regularity provides a basis for the MC to explore different flows, different moods. If poetry is essentially about the precise selection and arrangement of language, then hip hop may just be the best place to find it in today's music, if not in contemporary culture as a whole.

Nonetheless, the most popular rap often has the least to offer someone interested in hip-hop poetics. Rap veteran Ice-T was defending the sanctity of rap's tradition when he called out the hip-hop newcomer Soulja Boy (he of the ubiquitous 2007 hit "Crank That [Soulja Boy]"). In an explicative-laced tirade, he accused the teenage rapper of "single-handedly ruining hip hop" by producing "garbage" rap with little substance. Soulja Boy responded, as one might expect, by cracking on Ice-T's age and his lack of relevance. But he also issued a provocative challenge: "You don't like the way hip hop is, then change it." Soulja Boy and the loose association of predominantly southern artists that make up the culture of crunk, snap music, and other forms of club rap are doing just that. "Crank That" is nobody's idea of a hip-hop poetic masterpiece: It is bass heavy with simple melodies and even simpler lyrics. It was a worldwide hit that had people yelling out "Superman!" from Oakland to Auckland. It popularized a new dance craze and sparked a host of discussions about the song's distinctive terminology. What stands out most about the lyrics are the energy of Soulja Boy's delivery and the vocal quality of his southern slang. The less said about the poetry, the better. Far from being a defect, however, the absence of poetic innovation seems by design. Clever wordplay and complex flows would have weighed the song down. It was a hit precisely because Soulja Boy didn't try to make the song anything other than what it was.

The pleasure derived from poetically sophisticated rhymes is not necessarily greater than that which can be gained from a commercially successful but less literary track. The difference is that poetically minded MCs demand their audience's participation to make meaning out of their words. Unlike a hot beat, a great poetic line is not always readily apparent. As we've seen in the preceding chapters, rap's poetry enlists us in the process of making meaning: demanding that we cede the power of our imaginations to the MC's suggestion (in basic ways through imagery and in more extended ways through storytelling) and calibrate our emotional sensitivities to register those of the performance (through tonal shifts and emotional appeals on the level of voice). These complex poetic processes occur in a matter of seconds, often without our ever acknowledging them. Those who love hip hop are already nuanced, if largely unconscious, students of hip-hop poetics.

But while all rap fans know what makes a great verse, we're still developing a common vocabulary to talk about it with one another. As an art form, rap embodies a series of opposites: predictability and spontaneity, repetition and revision, order and chaos. These creative tensions help define the specific values and conventions that govern rap. To help bring us closer to a language for talking about rap as art, I offer what I'll call the Ten Rap Commandments of Poetry. I present them to you in closing with hopes they will inspire continued discussions on rap's complex poetics.

1. Rap Thrives on Rhythm, Never on Monotony

Rhythm is the foundation of rap, in the beats as well as in the rhymes. Rappers' flows, their distinctive vocal cadences, establish reciprocal relationships with the beat. MCs can rap a little behind, or a little ahead, they can use their voices as counterpoint, or they can simply ride the beat where it wants to take them. But they must always respect the integrity of the rhythm by not letting the overall performance slip into complete chaos and disharmony.

Yes, rap is repetitive: The beats are usually in 4/4 time, and the samples are often constructed on short, repeated riffs. However, the departure from established rhythm patterns is just as important as the patterns themselves. One of the reasons, for instance, that Tupac is considered by many to be one of the greatest MCs of all time is that he mastered the skill of satisfying his listeners' rhythmic expectations with his distinctive flow while still finding ways to surprise them with unexpected departures from that pattern.

2. Rhyme Is Rap's Reason for Being

Rhyme is one of the few givens in rap lyricism. An MC must satisfy convention—and the audience—by rhyming words in some kind of discernable pattern. That said, over the years MCs have conceived an increasing variety of ways to quench the audience's thirst for rhyme while expanding their own lyrical possibilities. In most old-school rap, rhymes fell at the end of lines; nowadays, one is just as likely to hear a rhyme in the middle of a line, or a string of rhymed lines in a row. Also, the definition of which words rhyme with one another has expanded from the narrow, perfect rhymes of the past to half rhymes and other aural analogues that satisfy the expectation of rhyme while allowing rappers a much wider expressive range.

3. Rappers Say New Things in Old Ways and Old Things in New Ways

It isn't enough for rappers simply to use a simile or a metaphor; to stand out they must provide some spark of ingenuity. One measure of an MC's skill is in his or her ability to breathe new life into old forms by finding original things to say or at least new ways of talking about old things. For those rappers who continue to rehash old themes—the "money, cash, hos" Jay-Z once rapped about—the challenge is to find distinctive ways of addressing them, be it through an original metaphor or some other lyrical innovation.

4. Rap Values Clarity

This, in part, is why rap's relation to literary poetry is closer than that of many other forms of popular lyric. Rap wants to be understood. Mick Jagger intentionally slurs his way through "Rough Justice," while Eminem clearly enunciates every word on "Stan." Clarity might just be the reason rap is so often targeted for censorship. It doesn't hide behind the music; it almost always comes through loud and clear.

5. Verbal Dexterity Is the Best Measure of a Rapper's Virtuosity

Wordplay, the creative application of rap figures and forms, is only the most obvious test of a rapper's skill. The best measure of virtuosity, however, might be sublinguistic, the manipulation of syllables and sounds. "I like being read," Rakim explains. "The way you do that is by having a lot of words, a lot of syllables, different types of words." This requires ingenious poetry, but it also requires mastery of physical qualities like breath control and articulation.

6. Voice Matters in Rap

The voice is a rapper's instrument. Not all instruments, however, are created equal. Rap has its share of great voices:
Chuck D, Tupac, Biggie, Q-Tip, Lauryn Hill. It also has its
share of strange, limited, or undistinguished ones. Regardless
of the tonal quality, though, voice matters. As KRS-One explains, "Rappers should always remember that their own
voices are the true essence of Rap music, and it is that
essence that gives the Rapper life." More often than not,
those rappers consistently listed among the greatest of all
time are also gifted with tremendous vocal instruments. A
great voice does not guarantee success, nor does a grating one
damn one to obscurity.

7. Thematic Development Is Essential in Shaping Rap's Lyrical Content

A rapper who spits a series of disconnected couplets is generally considered less skillful than one who can develop multiple facets of a particular theme or idea. In its most evolved
form, this takes the shape of narrative—rap storytelling. It
could also mean sixteen bars on your lyrical skill or your opponent's weakness. It could mean an abstract idea refracted
through a series of images and figurative constructions. Regardless of the specifics, rap audiences expect a sense of cohe-
sion and wholeness from a rhyme.

8. Rap Is No Joke, But It Can Definitely Be Funny

Rap's image in the popular imagination is dominated by aggression: young black men talking about guns, drugs, and violence. Comedy would seem to have little place. Mobb Deep's
Prodigy best expressed this attitude of straight-faced menace

when he rapped on "Eye for an Eye," "I might crack a smile, but ain't a damn thing funny." That said, much rap has an irrepressible sense of humor. Its wit is often displayed in conjunction with its aggression—sometimes to undercut it even to the point of parody; other times to render it more sinister still, as in the chillingly lighthearted way that the Notorious B.I.G. sometimes rapped about death. Without a doubt, rap has its share of comedians, from clown princes like Flavor Flav and Ol' Dirty Bastard to slow-flowing, sardonic wits like Too Short and Snoop Dogg. Hip hop's humor shares in the spirit of the tragicomic, an essential force behind black American cultural expression, from the blues to the dozens.

9. Rap Can Be High Concept or Low Concept, But It's Never No Concept

For some hip-hop purists the astounding popularity of D4L's 2006 chart-topping single "Laffy Taffy" spelled the end of hip hop as we know it. How could such a simplistic and, well, *dumb* song ever become so popular? What happened to lyrics with meaning? The fact is that rap has always catered to a broad range of tastes. For every song like "The Message" there was a "Fat Boys." "Laffy Taffy" was recorded for the clubs—night clubs, dance clubs, strip clubs. Yes, it was low concept, but it *had a concept,* and within those shockingly limited constraints, it was a tremendous success.

High-concept raps—not to be confused necessarily with high-*quality* raps—are those that aspire to grand expressive range and purpose. That purpose may be to express sociopolitical messages (like so-called conscious rappers), or it may be to experiment with new lyrical forms (such as Immortal Technique's nine-and-half-minute lyrical horror story, "Dance with the Devil") or to set a lyrical challenge for oneself (like

Long Beach's Crooked I did when he came up with *The Dream Tapes*, a series of a cappella freestyles he spit onto a bedside tape recorder just after waking up in the morning). Rap is at its weakest when it does away with a clear concept, an articulate vision of order and purpose. For rap to thrive, an audience has to be able to hear in the lyrics the reason that the rapper picked up the microphone.

10. Rap Relies on Originality and Recycling, All at Once

Kool G Rap once warned that "biters are wanted like animals hunted." Biting another MC's style is the greatest crime a lyricist can commit, and yet rap could not exist had it not borrowed heavily from other art forms. That both of these things can be true is rap's fundamental paradox. From the musical sampling that often comprises hip-hop tracks to the lyrical "biting" that makes direct use of other people's words, rap is filled with things that originally belonged to others. So what separates creative adaptation from outright theft? The answer lies in rap's originality.

As an art form, rap relies on repetition—but repetition with a difference. Its creative process consists of MCs taking ready-made things that are close at hand and transforming them to fit the pattern of their unique artistic vision. While biters might simply copy someone's flow, or even try to pass off someone else's lyrics as their own, true MCs have the ability to make what they take from others into something all their own.

You may disagree with some of these claims. If you do, that's fine with me because it's only in heated discussions among rappers, writers, and hip-hop fans that we'll finally appreciate hip hop's poetry. None of the commandments that I've laid down is fixed; they are open to addition, revision, or rejection. They belong to every MC, but most of all they belong to the rest of us. As active listeners, we can affect rap's values by what we choose to hear. Even more important, we can shape these values—and with them, the future of rap itself—by becoming better listeners, sophisticated enough to comprehend rap's finest examples of lyrical invention and, in turn, to inspire the best MCs to continued heights of lyrical greatness. Will rap stand the test of time? The answer is in the book of rhymes.

Acknowledgments

THIS BOOK IS the product of many hours spent listening to hip hop, reading poetry, and talking about both—sometimes separately and sometimes together. The idea for *Book of Rhymes* was born during late-night listening sessions with my friend Andrew DuBois. Many of the insights in this book are also his. We both had the privilege of studying poetry with Helen Vendler, a magnificent teacher; her influence is apparent throughout. I also wish to thank Henry Louis Gates, Jr., Cornel West, Werner Sollors, Larry Buell, and John Callahan, all great mentors who have shaped my thinking about literature and culture.

Robert Guinsler, my agent, worked tirelessly to find the best home for this book. We found it at Basic*Civitas*. I wish to thank all the folks there—in particular, Chris Greenberg, the editor who originally took on the project, and Brandon Proia, the editor who saw the book through to publication, pushing for my best.

Claremont McKenna College offered me tremendous support while I was writing this book, through summer grants and a year-long research leave. Thanks to my Literature Department colleagues, past and present, for their encouragement: Audrey Bilger, Robert Faggen, John Farrell, Tobias Gregory, Seth Lobis, Ann Meyer, Jim Morrison, and Nick Warner. Thanks also to my colleagues in Black Studies, in particular: Dipa Basu, Hal Fairchild, Eric Hurley, Val Thomas, and Sheila Walker.

My friend and former student Max Lipset dedicated himself to this book like it was his own, offering the kinds of indispensable insights and suggestions that only a true hip-hop head could provide. I'm deeply indebted to him.

A number of other students also informed and inspired this work, from the members of my Twentieth-Century Black Poetics seminars to the students with whom I've talked about hip hop over the years, both inside and outside of the classroom. I thank all of them, but particularly: Erika Andraca, Ryan Avanzado, Brentt Baltimore, Severine Beaulieu, Teo Bennett, J. R. Bonhomme-Isaiah, Monique Cadle, Jordan Crumley, Lisette Farve, Antoine Grant, Griffin Halpern, Moose Halpern, Kazumi Igus, Steven Kim, Ryan Larsen, Salim Lemelle, Brendan Loper, Candice McCray, Ryan Gaines McDonald, Courtney Moffett-Bateau, Kiki Namikas, Winston Owens, Aleksis Psychas, Ritika Puri, Glen Rice, Ava Robinson, Kevin Shih, Simon Shogry, Paul Snell, Jin Tan, Ramón Torres, Koko Umoren, Candace Valenzuela, Sean Abu Wilson, and Terrell Whitfield.

Many people have inspired, challenged, and sustained me in my love of hip hop and poetry over the years. In particular, I wish to thank: Jabari Asim, Emily Bernard, Jonathan Brent, the Bredie family (Jos, Carmen, Nick, and Chris), HV Claytor, Sam Davis III (hipolitics.com in '09!), Derek Foster, Justin Francis (big thanks for the author photo), Chris Freeberg, David Gallagher, Cruz Gamboa, Wil Haygood, R. Scott Heath, Jim von der Heydt, John L. Jackson, Jr., Shani Jamila, Ayinde Jean-Baptiste, Romulus Johnson, Mike Lipset, Ayanna Lonian, Megan McDaniel, James Miller, Kevin Merida, Martha Nadell, Lonnae O'Neal Parker, Renée Ann Richardson, Rossi Russell, Jonathan Tambiah, Ulrica Wilson, and David Yaffe. A special thanks to those who read and commented on all or part of the manuscript, including: Malik Ali, Glenda Carpio, Maggie Fromm, Michaeljulius Idani, Dimitry Elias Léger, Jim Morrison, Lance Rutledge, Sarah Spain Shelton, and Jason Shelton.

It is a pleasure and a responsibility to write about hip hop at a time when so many gifted writers and scholars are already doing it so well. I wish to acknowledge a few of them here: H. Samy Alim, James Bernard, Jon Caramanica, Jeff Chang, William Jelani Cobb, Brian Coleman, Kyle Dargan, Michael Gonzales, Bakari Kitwana, Adam Krims, Ferentz Lafargue, Adam Mansbach, Joan Morgan, Mark Anthony Neal, Imani Perry, Gwendolyn Pough, Marcus Reeves, Kelefa Sanneh, James G. Spady, Oliver Wang, and S. Craig Watkins. And, of course, none of us would have anything to write about without the many MCs—underground, aboveground, and in between—who are keeping hip hop very much alive. There are far too many artists to name, so I'll just say, "Thanks to hip hop."

Finally, I thank my family for their love and support: my mother, Jane Bradley, and her partner, Kenny Wine; my late grandparents Iver and Jane Bradley, who taught me at home until high school; my brother, Jack Meyer, and his wife, Sarah Coleman-Meyer; my beautiful aunts LaVerne Tucker, Kathy Terry, and Catherine Terry; my late father, Jim Terry, and my stepmother, Beth Terry; Chuck Meyer and Sunny Meyer; my brother- and sister-in-law, Jason Shelton and Sarah Spain Shelton; and my in-laws, Bill and Mary Spain. Most of all, I wish to thank Anna, my remarkable wife, closest friend, and best critic. Her love sustains me.

Notes

RAP POETRY 101

xiv **"An enormous amount of creative energy":** Jeff Chang, *Can't Stop, Won't Stop: A History of the Hip-Hop Generation* (New York: St. Martin's Press, 2005), 82–83.

xiv **"Rap was the final conclusion":** KRS-One, *Ruminations* (New York: Welcome Rain Publishers, 2003), 217.

xvii **"aspires towards the condition of music":** Walter Pater, "The School of Giorgione" (1877), reprinted in *Selected Writings of Walter Pater*, ed. Harold Bloom (New York: Columbia University Press, 1974), 55.

xvii **"The lyric poem always walks the line":** Edward Hirsch, *How to Read a Poem and Fall in Love with Poetry* (New York: Harcourt Brace, 1999), 10.

ONE Rhythm

4   **"I can go to Japan":** David Ma, "Bear Witness: Dilated
Peoples' Evidence Testifies to Hip-Hop's Longevity," *Wax
Poetics*, No. 26, December-January 2008, 55.

5   **"Poetic forms are like that":** Paul Fussell, *Poetic Meter and
Poetic Form* (New York: McGraw-Hill, Inc., 1979), 126.

5   **from a groan to a sonnet is a straight line:** Cleanth Brooks
and Robert Penn Warren, *Conversations on the Craft of Poetry*
(New York: Holt, Rinehart & Winston, 1961).

5   **"an elaboration of the rhythms of common speech":**
William Butler Yeats, "Modern Poetry" (1936), reprinted in
Essays and Introductions (London: Macmillan, 1961), 499–500.

5   **"Music only needs a pulse":** The RZA, *The Wu-Tang
Manual: Enter the 36 Chambers*, Vol. 1 (New York: Riverhead,
2005), 204.

6   **"The beat of the heart seems to be basic":** Robert Frost,
"Conversations on the Craft of Poetry," reprinted in *Robert
Frost on Writing* (New Brunswick, NJ: Rutgers University
Press, 1973), 155–156.

6   **"inspire that feeling in an MC":** The RZA, 208.

7   **"Well, initially, [I would] probably just [write] my rhymes":**
Andrew Mason and Dale Coachman, "The Metamorphosis:

Ever-Evolving Q-Tip Emerges with New Sounds," *Wax Poetics*, No. 28, April 2008, 93.

8   **"what results when the natural rhythmical movements":** Fussell, 4.

10   **"Today one almost hesitates to say":** Timothy Steele, *Missing Measures: Modern Poetry and the Revolt Against Meter* (Fayetteville: University of Arkansas Press, 1990), 281.

12   **"rap pretty much is subservient to the beat":** H. Samy Alim, *Roc the Mic Right: The Language of Hip Hop Culture* (New York: Routledge, 2006), 96.

13   **"Just to hear the bass was like everything":** Jim Fricke and Charlie Ahearn, *Yes Yes Y'all: The Experience Music Project Oral History of Hip-Hop's First Decade* (New York: Da Capo Press, 2002), 43.

14   **"The Kool Herc style at the time":** Fricke and Ahearn, 74.

15   **"MCs were elevating the art of rhyme":** Marcus Reeves, *Somebody Scream! Rap Music's Rise to Prominence in the Aftershock of Black Power* (New York: Faber and Faber, Inc., 2008).

15   **"Every subsequent generation of MCs":** William Jelani Cobb, *To the Break of Dawn: A Freestyle on the Hip Hop Aesthetic* (New York: New York University Press, 2007), 47.

17 **"I was 12, the same age my oldest daughter":** Lonnae
O'Neal Parker, "Why I Gave Up on Hip-Hop," *Washington
Post*, October 15, 2006, B1.

19 **"Blacks alone didn't invent poetics":** Robert B. Stepto and
Michael S. Harper, "Study and Experience: An Interview with
Ralph Ellison," 1976, reprinted in *Conversations with Ralph
Ellison*, ed. Maryemma Graham and Amritjit Singh (Oxford:
University of Mississippi Press, 1995), 330.

22 **"You may not realize it":** Robert Frost, "The Way There"
(1958), *Robert Frost: Collected Poems, Prose, and Plays* (New
York: Library of America), 847.

25 **"If he uses ten syllables in a line, I'm going to use fifteen":**
Jon Caramanica, "Bun B," *The Believer*, June-July 2006.

29 **"Rhythm science is not so much a new language":** Paul D.
Miller, *Rhythm Science* (Cambridge, MA: MIT Press, 2004),
72.

32 **"an individual time signature":** Cobb, 87.

37 **"What you find with a lot of rappers":** "Dead Cert," *The
Observer*, April 25, 2004.

39 **"I think a lot of artists that rap":** "Twista: Fast Talk, Slow
Climb," MTVNews.com, 2005.

40 **"If, in rap, rhythm is more significant":** Simon Frith,
Performing Rites: On the Value of Popular Music (Cambridge,
MA: Harvard University Press, 1998), 175.

41   **"My style of writing":** Tom Breihan, "Status Ain't Hood Interviews Rakim," *Village Voice*, June 6, 2006.

42   **"I had long had haunting my ear":** Gerard Manley Hopkins, July 24, 1866, journal entry, reprinted in *Gerard Manley Hopkins: Poems and Prose* (New York: Penguin, 1953), 185.

43   **"Once I figure out in my mind":** Caramanica, "Bun B."

44   **"In early hip-hop":** The RZA, 108.

47   **"Crafting a good flow is like doing a puzzle":** Stic.man, *The Art of Emcee-ing* (New York: Boss Up, Inc., 2005), 53.

two **Rhyme**

50   **"Along with word choice and sound patterns":** Frances Mayes, *The Discovery of Poetry: A Field Guide to Reading and Writing* (New York: Harcourt Brace, 2001), 167.

52   **"Where there is no similarity, there is no rhyme":** Alfred Corn, *The Poem's Heartbeat: A Manual of Prosody* (New York: Story Line Press, 1997), 77.

54   **"The coincidence of sound in a pair of rhymes":** Corn, 75.

54   **"MCing, to me":** Common, "The Greatest MCs of All Time," MTV.com, 2006.

55   **"The search for a rhyme-word":** Steve Kowit, *In the Palm of Your Hand: The Poet's Portable Workshop* (Gardiner, ME: Tilbury House Publishers, 1995), 161.

55   **"The imagination wants its limits":** Derek Walcott, *Conversations with Derek Walcott* (Jackson: University of Mississippi Press, 1995), 105.

58   **"Perfection of the rhymes":** James G. Spady, *Street Conscious Rap* (Philadelphia: Black History Museum Press, 1999), 550.

59   **"Some artists use line after line":** Emcee Escher and Alex Rappaport, *The Rapper's Handbook: A Guide to Freestyling, Writing Rhymes, and Battling* (New York: Flocabulary LLC, 2006), 28.

69   **"a constraint to express many things otherwise":** John Milton, *Selected Prose* (Columbia: University of Missouri Press, 1985), 404.

69   **"popularitie of Rime creates":** Thomas Campion, "Observations in the Art of English Poesie" (1602), reprinted in *Renascence Edition* (Eugene: University of Oregon, 1998).

70   **"Staying in the unconscious frame of mind":** Benjamin Hedin, *Studio A: The Bob Dylan Reader* (New York: W. W. Norton & Company, 2004), 215.

70   **"It gives you a thrill to rhyme something":** Hedin, 215.

79   **"When I started out as a DJ":** Fricke and Ahearn, 79.

79   **"So different DJs started embellishing":** Fricke and Ahearn, 79.

82   **"When we first started rhyming":** Fricke and Ahearn, 74.

THREE **Wordplay**

87   **"shunned expressions of disposable people":** Cobb, 6.

87   **"Thus if these [vernacular] poets":** Ralph Ellison, "Some
Questions and Some Answers," *The Collected Essays of Ralph
Ellison* (New York: Random House, 1994), 295.

87   **"When I was young":** *And You Don't Stop: 30 Years of Hip
Hop*, VH1, 2004.

87   **"Hip hop has so much power":** "Resurrection: Common
Walks," PopMatters music interview, September 21,
2005.

87   **"The great body of Negro slang":** Ellison, "What These
Children Are Like," 555.

88   **"A language comes into existence":** James Baldwin, "If Black
English Isn't a Language, Then Tell Me, What Is?" *New York
Times*, July 29, 1979.

88   **"People may look at it like":** Anthony DeCurtis, "Wu-Tang
Family Values," *Rolling Stone*, July 24, 1997.

90   **"Rather than being about experience":** Mayes, 427.

90   **"It's just a vehicle":** H. Samy Alim, "Interview with Ras
Kass," James G. Spady, et al, *The Global Cipha: Hip Hop
Culture and Consciousness* (Philadelphia: Black History
Museum Press, 2006), 241.

90 **"defamiliarizes words":** Hirsch, 12.

91 **"It's one thing to say 'I sell bricks, I sell bricks'":** John
Caramanica, "Keep on Pushin'," *Mass Appeal* 39, 72.

92 **"All poetry implies the destruction":** Ellison, "Society,
Morality, and and the Novel," 702.

FOUR Style

122 **"We develop schemas":** Daniel J. Levitin, *This Is Your Brain on
Music: The Science of a Human Obsession* (New York: Penguin,
2007), 117.

124 **"history, geography, and genre all at once":** Adam Krims,
Rap Music and the Poetics of Identity (New York: Cambridge
University Press, 2000), 48.

125 **"a dynamic process":** Ellison, "Going to the Territory,"
612.

126 **"Hip-hop is a beautiful culture":** Richard Cromlein, "Mos
Def Wants Blacks to Take Back Rock Music," *Los Angeles
Times*, December 28, 2004.

128 **"Queens rappers have a special style":** *And You Don't Stop.*

132 **"Technically, Tupac wasn't a great rapper":** *The Vibe History
of Hip-Hop* (New York: Three Rivers Press, 1999), 93.

133 **"Biggie's gonna win hands down":** *The Art of 16 Bars*, Image
Entertainment, 2005.

135 **"A distinct voice tone is the identity":** KRS-One, 247.

136 **"I suspect that the freshest and most engaging poems":** Ted
Kooser, The Poetry Home Repair Manual: Practical Advice for
Beginning Poets (Lincoln: University of Nebraska Press, 2005), 14.

136 **"the language of a poem is constitutive of its ideas":** Terry
Eagleton, How to Read a Poem (Malden, MA: Blackwell
Publishing), 2.

137 **"It's like if you wanna rap like Jay[-Z]":** Jake Brown, Kanye
West in the Studio: Beats Down! Money Up! (Phoenix: Amber
Books Publishing), 40–41.

140 **"I didn't know what I was doing":** 50 Cent and Kris Ex,
From Pieces to Weight: Once Upon a Time in Southside Queens
(New York: MTV Books, 2005), 163.

141 **"I wasn't a good writer":** And You Don't Stop.

141 **"Obviously, I was young":** Eminem biography,
eminemonline.com.

142 **"My style of writing":** Breihan, "Status Ain't Hood Interview:
Rakim."

142 **"But as far as what makes me unique":** Cedric Muhammad,
"Hip-Hop Fridays: Exclusive Q&A with Ludacris,"
blackelectorate.com, May 9, 2003.

143 **"I was speeding":** Kelefa Sanneh, "Uneasy Lies the Head,"
New York Times, November 19, 2006.

144 **"I honestly never sat down":** Caramanica, "Bun B."

144 **"Style is almost unconscious":** William Butler Yeats, *Yeats' Poetry, Drama, and Prose* (New York: W. W. Norton & Company), 308.

144 **"characteristic words and images":** Mayes, 375.

145 **"Today we take rhyme styles for granted":** Brian Coleman, *Check the Technique: Liner Notes for Hip-Hop Junkies* (New York: Villard, 2007), 91.

149 **"I wish there could be some control of it":** Ellison, "Ellison: Exploring the Life of a Not So Visible Man," Hollie I. West (1973), published in *Conversations with Ralph Ellison*, eds. Maryemma Graham and Amritjit Singh (Jackson: University of Mississippi Press, 1995), 251.

149 **"I'm not a separatist":** Ellison, *Conversations*, 235.

151 **"Writing for Biz was in a whole different style":** Coleman, 37.

153 **"I really pride myself on being a vocalist":** Rikky Rooksby, *Lyrics: Writing Better Words for Your Songs* (San Francisco: Backbeat Books, 2006), 107.

FIVE Storytelling

159 **"I come from a literary background":** Ken Capobianco, "Lupe Fiasco Accepts the Outsider Label as a Positive Rap," *Boston Globe*, November 13, 2006.

160 **"It was almost like a diary":** Coleman, 419.

163 **"The first is the poet talking to himself":** T. S. Eliot, "The Three Voices of Poetry" (1955), reprinted in *Lewis Turco's The Book of Forms: A Handbook of Poetics* (Hanover, NH: University Press of New England, 2000), 120.

164 **"poems spoken by a character":** John Drury, *The Poetry Dictionary* (Cincinnati, OH: Writer's Digest Books, 2006), 78–79.

164 **"On 99 percent of the songs":** Spady, "Interview with Pharoahe Monch," *The Global Cipha*, 141.

165 **"In both Stagolee and the dramatic monologue":** Cecil Brown, *Stagolee Shot Billy* (Cambridge, MA: Harvard University Press, 2003), 221.

166 **"It may be of great interest to discover":** "Persona," *The New Princeton Encyclopedia of Poetry and Poetics* (Princeton, NJ: Princeton University Press, 1993), 900.

166 **"The same respect is often not extended to hip-hop artists":** David Banner, "David Banner's Speech to Congress Over Hip Hop Lyrics," ballerstatus.com, September 27, 2007.

167 **"In hip-hop, the whole 'keep it real'":** Jay-Z, *Stop Smiling* No. 33, 2007, 45–46.

167 **"I'd say 60 percent is really":** Jason Newman, "Everybody Plays the Fool (Sometimes): Devin the Dude is Hip-Hop's

Court Jester," *Wax Poetics*, No. 28, December-January 2008, 52.

172 **"Narrative is a verbal presentation"**: "Narrative Poetry," *New Princeton Encyclopedia*, 814.

six Signifying

176 **"The ability of the live performer"**: Derek Collins, *Master of the Game: Competition and Performance in Greek Poetry* (Cambridge, MA: Harvard University Press, 2005), x–xi.

177 **"People compare rap to other genres of music"**: Cobb, 79.

177 **"I don't write, homie"**: "Lil Wayne Interview," ign.com, June 5, 2004.

178 **"I could be at my happiest moment"**: ign.com.

178 **"When you write a rhyme"**: *The Art of 16 Bars*.

178 **"All the lyrics on there were written down"**: Coleman, 384.

179 **"I think in freestyle"**: Spady, "Interview with N.O.R.E. a.k.a. Noreaga," 92.

181 **"the rhetorical principle in Afro-American vernacular discourse"**: Henry Louis Gates, Jr., *The Signifying Monkey: A Theory of African-American Literary Criticism* (New York: Oxford University Press, 1989), 44.

188 **"In hip hop—and inside the broken histories of black men in America"**: Cobb, 80.

190 **"'Signifying Rapper' . . . is a tour de force"**: William Eric Perkins, *Droppin' Science: Critical Essays on Rap Music and Hip Hop Culture* (Philadelphia: Temple University Press, 1996), 17.

191 **"an outsized hero that has more sex"**: *And You Don't Stop*.

191 **"The persona overshadows"**: *And You Don't Stop*.

191 **"Exaggerated and invented boasts"**: Robin D. G. Kelley, *Yo' Mama's Disfunktional! Fighting the Culture Wars in Urban America* (Boston: Beacon Press, 1997), 37–38.

192 **"When my dad would teach me lessons"**: Coleman, 241.

195 **"Commercial success and artistic integrity"**: Stic.man, 15.

196 **"I just think in general our society limits"**: Byron Hurt, *Hip Hop: Beyond Beats and Rhymes* (2007).

196 **"is allowed to be introspective"**: Scott Thill, "Eminem vs. Robert Frost," Salon.com, March 18, 2004.

199 **"to start with the stereotype"**: Ralph Ellison, *Shadow & Act* (New York: Random House, 1964), 43.

199 **"Rap is really funny, man"**: *Vibe*, 93.

200 **"Hip hop doesn't place as high a premium on irony":** Cobb, 24.

201 **"The blues is an impulse":** Ellison, 129.

201 **"Timeless music":** Jay-Z, *XXL*, 2006.

202 **"All I know is I wanted to feel a certain way":** Jason Genegabus, "Mos Def: From Film to Fashion to Music, He's a Tough Act to Follow," *Honolulu Star-Bulletin*, February 18, 2005.

EPILOGUE

209 **"The way you do that":** Tom Breihan, "Status Ain't Hood Interviews Rakim," VillageVoice.com, June 6, 2006.

210 **"Rappers should always remember":** KRS-One, 247.

Index

The Rime of the Ancient Mariner
(Coleridge), 20, 21
Roach, Max, 43
Robinson, Sylvia, 16
"Rollin' with Saget" (Kennedy),
198
Rolling Stone magazine, 67–68,
132
Roots, 37, 126, 150, 178
Ross, Rick, 21
Roth, Asher, 57
"Rough Justice" (Jagger), 209
Run DMC, 22, 113, 116, 125,
140, 190
Runnin' Off at da Mouth (Twista),
38
RZA, 5–6, 44, 146, 164

Saddler, Joseph. *See* Grandmaster
Flash
Salon.com, 196
Samberg, Andy, 198
Santana, Juelz, 98, 115–116
"S.A.N.T.A.N.A." (Santana),
115–116
Saturday Night Live, 198
Scansion, 9–10
Scat, 43
Schoolly D, 189 190
Scorpio, 82
Seinfeld, 200
"Sekou Story" (Nas), 166, 173
Senneh, Kelefa, 143
Shakespeare, William, 9–10, 93,
97, 116, 148
Shakur, Tupac (Tupac; Pac),
67–68, 71, 131–133,
134–135, 166, 168–169,
197, 208, 210
Shanté, Roxanne, 128, 151–152
Sha-Rock, 13
Shelley, Percy Bysshe, 89

"She's Alive" (Andre 3000), 171
Shock-G, 133
Shyne, 134
Signature style, 143, 148. *See also*
Style
Signifying, 181–201
and boasting, 193–194
and braggadocio, 181–182,
187–189
and comedy, 198–201
and commercialism, 194–196
definition of, 181
and dissing, 186–187
and dozens, 181
and gangsta rap, 189–193
and invulnerability, 196–198
and kenning, 182–183
and O'Neil vs. Bryant,
184–185
and parody, 198–199
and toasts, 181
See also Battle rap; Cipher;
Swagger
The Signifying Monkey (Gates),
181
"The Signifying Monkey" (toast),
190
"The Signifying Rapper"
(Schoolly D), 190
Simile, 89, 92, 93–96
and tenor, 95
and vehicle, 95
See also Punning simile
"Simon Says" (Pharoahe
Monch), 61
Skelton, John, 75–76
Skeltonics, 76
Slant rhyme. *See* Imperfect
rhyme
"Sleazy Gynecologist" (Slick
Rick), 160
Slick Rick, 160, 166

and theft, 147
and unconscious mind,
144–145
and vernacular process,
125–126
and voice, 134–135
Sugar Hill Gang, 15, 16, 21,
80–81, 152, 160, 183
Sugar Hill Records, 16
Superhead. *See* Steffans, Karrine
"Super-rappin'" (Grandmaster
Flash and the Furious Five),
82
Swagger, 180–181. *See also*
Signifying
"Swagger Like Us" (Kanye West),
103
Swan, T. J., 49
Syllables, 25–26, 29, 40–42
"Sylvester's Dying Bed"
(Langston Hughes),
xxii–xxiii
Syncopation, 7

Tajai, 94, 95–96
Talent, 141
Technique, 134, 135–136
Tempo, 38–39
"Ten Crack Commandments"
(Notorious B.I.G.), 146
Ten Rap Commandments of
Poetry, 207–213
Tenor, and simile, 95
Territory, and style, 128
"Testify" (Common), 165–166
Theft, 147. *See also* Borrowing
Thematic development, 210
"This Can't Be Life" (Jay-Z), 137
Thomas, Dylan, 58
"Threats" (Jay-Z), 108
Toasts, 14, 181
Too Short, 199, 211

"Trade It All" (Fabolous), 76–77
Transformative rhyme (forced
rhyme), 71–73
Trigga Tha Gambler, 182–183
Tristram Shandy (Sterne), 171
"Triumph" (Wu-Tang Clan), 3
Troutman, Roger, 68
True rhyme. *See* Perfect rhyme
Tung Twista. *See* Twista
Tupac. *See* Shakur, Tupac
"Twinz" (Big Punisher), 68–69
Twista (Tung Twista), 38–39

"U.B.R. (Unauthorized Biography
of Rakim)" (Nas), 173
UGK, 144
Unconscious mind
and rhyme, 70
and style, 144–145
"Undying Love" (Nas), 165,
173–174
universalurban.com, 137

A *Valediction: Forbidding
Mourning* (Donne), 97
"Valse Hot" (Roach), 43
Vehicle, and simile, 95
Verbal dexterity, 209
Vernacular process, 24, 149
and style, 125–126
Village Voice, 142
Voice (as instrument), 210
Voice (of storyteller), 134–135,
162–166
and battle rap, 163
and braggadocio, 163
and first-person narrative, 162,
164–166

Walcott, Derek, 55
Warren, Robert Penn, 5
Washington Post, 17